STEAM
Locomotive
Projects & Ideas

Compiled by John Pryke

KALMBACH
BOOKS

Printed in the United States of America

03 04 05 06 07 08 09 10 11 12   10 9 8 7 6 5 4 3 2 1

Visit our Web site at http://kalmbachbooks.com
Secure online ordering available

Publisher's Cataloging-in-Publication
(Provided by Quality Books, Inc.)

Steam locomotive projects and ideas / compiled by John
  Pryke. — 1st ed.
    p. cm.
    Includes bibliographical references.
    ISBN 0-89024-400-6

    1. Railroads—Models.   I. Pryke, John.

TF197.S73 2003   625.1'961
                        QBI03-200589

Art director: Kristi Ludwig
Designer: Kory Beavers

Table of Contents

Preface

The Industrial Revolution introduced steam as a primary energy source. Factories used large steam engines to power machinery through a maze of shafts and belts. By the early 1800s, steam was applied to transportation: ships, tractors and railroads. The first railroad locomotives, like Stephenson's Rocket of 1829, had boilers to heat water and cylinders to power the wheels, but each design placed these components in different configurations. As the miles of track increased during the 1840s, a standard convention was established—a horizontal boiler with the firebox to the rear, and a smoke box and stack in front. Horizontal cylinders, under the smoke box, powered driving wheels under the boiler, whose weight provided added traction. A leading truck and eventually a trailing truck helped carry the weight of the cylinders and firebox respectively. Wood and, later, coal were used as fuel. By the 1860s, the standard passenger locomotive had a 4-4-0 wheel arrangement, while freight engines added more driving wheels for greater pulling power.

In the early 1900s, steam engines evolved rapidly in both size and power. New fuels like oil, and a second (and even a third) set of drivers were added to haul heavy trains. Many methods were used to increase efficiency, including pre-heating water before it entered the boiler, moving coal from the tender to the engine by automatic stokers, and adding small booster engines to trailing trucks to start trains.

The steam locomotive was a breathtaking piece of machinery, often more than 100 ft. long with many moving parts in its driving rods and valve gear. These behemoths thundered down the rails, raising clouds of smoke and belching deafening blasts of exhaust. They captured the attention of everyone that saw one, and sparked the desire to have a miniature model of a steam engine in men and boys alike.

The earliest models were made of cast iron. They were heavy and crude, and could be pulled along the floor with a string. In 1900, the "electric train" made its debut, and steam engines were soon added to train sets. By the late 1920s, the boys who played with these early models were growing up and demanding models built to exact scale with more realistic detail. Manufacturers immediately answered and, by the late 1930s, model steam engines were available in several sizes, from diminutive HO to the larger S and O scales.

In the years after World War II, the amount of detail on these models increased dramatically. New materials like pressure die-castings, hand assembled brass, and plastic moldings allowed for prototypical accuracy to satisfy the most demanding modeler. But times were changing and, as the mighty steam engine went to the scrap yards on prototype railroads, the modeler's interests shifted to diesels. By 1995 the hobby swarmed with low-cost diesels, and the only steam engines available were hand-assembled brass imports from the Far East. Although these made magnificent models, the price of brass had spiraled out of reach for the average model railroader, and steam engines became the exception rather than the rule on most layouts.

By the late 1990s, new plastics and assembly methods were developed, and a new generation of model steam engine was born. Offering the detailing of brass at a fraction of the cost, these plastic models heralded a rebirth of steam on many model railroad layouts.

This book contains some of the best articles written on model steam locomotives over the last decade. First, you will learn about the major components of a prototype steam engine and how it works, then enjoy a history of scale model steam engines. Following this introduction, the book's four sections will focus on:
- Detailing
- Kitbashing and Scratchbuilding
- Painting
- Maintenance and Performance.

By the time you have read this book, you will know how to make this new family of model steam engines as realistic as their prototypes, and discover why adding steam to your layout increases the fun of model railroading.

John Pryke
May 2003

STEAM Locomotives

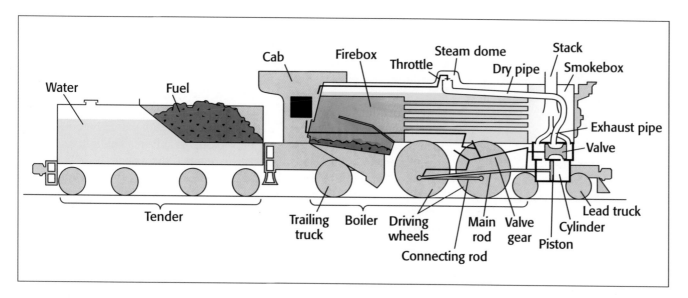

By George H. Drury

A steam locomotive uses steam from boiling water to power a set of driving wheels that move the engine forward or backward along the track. The boiler was the largest single part of a steamer, and held the water which was heated to make steam. Behind the boiler was the firebox where burning fuel (wood, coal, or oil) provided heat that was fed through the boiler in fire tubes and was exhausted through a smokebox and out a stack in front of the boiler.

Steam from the boiling water was captured in a steam dome on top of the boiler, and from there fed through a pipe to the cylinders below the smokebox. The cylinder moved back and forth and moved the driving wheels (under the boiler) through drive rods and connecting rods. The movement of the cylinder was controlled by additional rods (valve gear) that controlled the flow of steam to either end of the cylinder. The used steam was exhausted into the smokebox and used to blow the heat (and smoke) from the fire tubes out the stack. Behind the firebox was the cab where the engineer or fireman controlled the speed and direction of the

locomotive. The driving wheels, which propelled the locomotive were located under the boiler whose weight increased traction. A lead truck and trailing truck supported the cylinders and firebox, respectively. Immediately behind the engine was its tender which contained water (for the boiler) and fuel (for the firebox).

The steam locomotive was the major hauler on railroads from the very beginnings in the 1800s until about 1947. After that, in a short 10 years, all but a handful were scrapped or mounted on pedestals for the curious to examine. The last steam

Time Line: Significant innovations in steam locomotive technology

1830	First successful steam engine: Stephenson's Rocket	1845	American Standard (4-4-0) emerges with Ten-Wheeler (4-6-0) and Consolidation (2-8-0)	1904	First articulated 0-6-6-0 Stoker PRR test plant	1913	Booster engine	1920	USRA control ended March 1
		1835	Many new designs introduced; wooden and iron boilers	1900	Oil as fuel	1905	Superheater Wide firebox	1917	USRA control began Dec. 26

locomotives built for use in the United States were the 0-8-0 switchers of the Norfolk & Western, which were built in 1953 and scrapped in less than six years. In 1920, the peak, some 70,000 steam locomotives were operating at the same time; in all, perhaps 133,000 locos had been built by 1953.

Very early steam locomotives had two or four driving wheels and vertical or horizontal boilers with many varieties of driving mechanisms and valve gear. From 1845, the typical American design evolved with half-closed cab, two or four leading wheels, cowcatcher and headlight in front, and water supply and other piping usually exposed around the boiler.

Until the 1880s the common locomotive types were the American Standard or Eight-Wheeler, the Ten-Wheeler, and the Consolidation.

In the middle 1890s, every phase of railroad engineering became alive with improvements and since then locomotives of ever-increasing size were developed. The first important change was the use of the large firebox behind the driving wheels. It had usually been narrow and mounted between drivers up to this time. Related to this were the addition of trailing wheels, the need for stokers, and larger water supply systems.

The first great step in efficiency was the acceptance of the superheater around the years 1910-1914. Its hot steam in turn required piston-type valves instead of the old "D" slide valves. In the mid 1920s, efficiency became the principal concern and feedwater heaters, still-larger fireboxes, larger tenders, and also larger driving wheels on freight locomotives became the rule.

If the trend of the 1940s had continued, it looks as though simple articulated locomotives would have become the rule for freight service—the culmination of the struggle to build larger locomotives within the limitations of tunnel and bridge clearances.

No two steam locomotives alike?

When a new design was made for a steam locomotive, the usual practice was to build one or two trial engines. If the design proved successful, duplicate engines were then ordered in lots of a few or several score, depending on need. The entire group would be called a "class" on the owning railroad.

However, individual locomotives within a class are different, at least in minor and sometimes in important details. Locomotives were built and delivered over a period of months and changes were frequently made. There might be quite a few points of difference between the first and last engine of a class.

Later, as engines were shopped, more changes were made with the result that a locomotive was always changing and always different in some ways from others in its class.

Classification, nomenclature, and numbering

As locomotives developed there arose a need for a classification system, and number and arrangement of wheels worked out to be the best way to do it. The WHYTE system that was eventually settled on seems obvious, but it was preceded by others.

Baldwin Locomotives Works, for example, classified its locomotives with a numeral denoting the total number of wheels under the locomotive, a fraction indicating trailing and lead trucks ($\frac{1}{4}$ for trailing truck and lead truck; $\frac{1}{3}$ for trailing truck but no lead truck), and a letter giving the number of driving axles (B for 1, C for 2, D for 3, etc.). A Pacific was classed 12-$\frac{1}{4}$-D, for example.

A clearer, easier system was developed by Frederick Methven Whyte, a New York Central mechanical engineer. Numerals represented the number of wheels in each group, starting at the front end: lead truck, drivers, trailing truck. For articulated locomotives a numeral was used for each group of drivers, The numerals were separated by hyphens.

Most wheel arrangements were given names derived from the first user of that wheel arrangement.

Some railroads chose their own names for wheel arrangements, either officially or unofficially. New York Central, which constantly reminded passengers that it was the Water Level Route, designated its 4-8-2s Mohawks, not Mountains, and its 4-8-4s were Niagaras, not Northerns.

The 4-8-4 had more names than any other type. Memories of the War Between The States were still fresh in 1930 when Nashville, Chattanooga & St. Louis ("The Dixie Line") chose Dixie instead of Northern for its 4-8-4s; Richmond, Fredericksburg & Potomac called its 4-8-4s Generals and Governors and named them individually for confederate generals and Virginia governors. Local rivalry may be responsible for 2-8-4s being

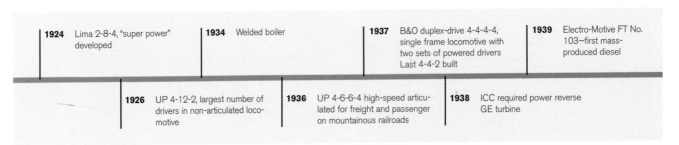

| 1924 | Lima 2-8-4, "super power" developed | 1934 | Welded boiler | 1937 | B&O duplex-drive 4-4-4-4, single frame locomotive with two sets of powered drivers Last 4-4-2 built | 1939 | Electro-Motive FT No. 103—first mass-produced diesel |

| 1926 | UP 4-12-2, largest number of drivers in non-articulated locomotive | 1936 | UP 4-6-6-4 high-speed articulated for freight and passenger on mountainous railroads | 1938 | ICC required power reverse GE turbine |

known as Limas on the Boston & Maine—they were Berkshires on the parallel Boston & Albany. During World War II anti-Japanese sentiment caused some railroads to rename their Mikados to MacArthurs.

Occasionally railroads renamed enlarged or improved versions of a wheel arrangement. The New Haven, for example, introduced its 3-cylinder 4-8-2s as the New Haven type, and the Atlantics built for Milwaukee Road's *Hiawatha* were dubbed the Milwaukee type. Such names seldom stuck.

Railroad classes

Railroads needed a convenient way to refer to groups of similar locomotives. Most roads eventually assigned a letter more or less arbitrarily to each wheel arrangement, usually with a number to note successive groups or different sizes of a type, and sometimes with a letter after the number to indicate variations.

Other roads chose a letter or two to abbreviate the common name of the type. One of the hazards is that several names start with the same letter.

Occasionally railroads assigned the same letter to two types. On the Milwaukee Road, for instance, classes F1 through F5 were 4-6-2s and F6 and F7 were 4-6-4s. Other roads—Santa Fe, for example—skipped letters entirely and simply referred to locomotives by number groups: the 1950 class, the 3700 class.

Some railroads used an "s" in their locomotive classifications to indicate superheating. Well-known examples are Southern Railway Ps-4 and Pennsylvania Railroad K4s Pacifics.

The Whyte Classification System		
Type	**Name**	
0-4-0	Four-wheel switcher	OO
0-6-0	Six-wheel switcher	OOO
0-8-0	Eight-wheel switcher	OOOO
0-10-2	Union	OOOOOo
2-4-2	Columbia	–oOOo
2-6-0	Mogul	–oOOO
2-6-2	Prairie	–oOOOo
2-8-0	Consolidation	–oOOOO
2-8-2	Mikado	–oOOOOo
2-8-4	Berkshire	–oOOOOoo
2-10-0	Decapod	–oOOOOO
2-10-2	Santa Fe	–oOOOOOo
2-10-4	Texas	–oOOOOOoo
2-6-6-6	Allegheny	–oOOO OOOooo
2-8-8-4	Yellowstone	–oOOOO OOOOoo
4-4-0	American, Eight-Wheeler	–ooOO
4-4-2	Atlantic	–ooOOo
4-4-4	Jubilee	–ooOOoo
4-6-0	Ten-Wheeler	–ooOOO
4-6-2	Pacific	–ooOOOo
4-6-4	Hudson	–ooOOOoo
4-8-0	Twelve-Wheeler	–ooOOOO
4-8-2	Mountain	–ooOOOOo
4-8-4	Northern	–ooOOOOoo
4-10-0	Mastodon	–ooOOOOO
4-10-2	Southern Pacific, Overland	–ooOOOOOo
4-12-2	Union Pacific	–ooOOOOOOo
4-6-6-4	Challenger	–ooOOO OOOoo
4-8-8-4	Big Boy	–ooOOOO OOOOoo

There were many ways to designate subclasses and sub-subclasses: numbers, letters (both lower-case and small capitals), and even fractions.

Numbering

In the beginning, or at least when numbers replaced names, railroads numbered their locomotives in sequence as they acquired them. When all the locomotives were 4-4-0s of about the same size it didn't make much difference. As different types of locomotives developed and locomotive fleets grew in size, many railroads found it useful to assign numbers so that engines that were alike had adjacent numbers, so that all the 80s were 2-6-0s, and all the 90s 2-8-0s, or all the passenger engines were 300s and all the freight engines 400s. Some railroads used different number series for divisions or subsidiaries. A few railroads continued the older practice, and some reassigned numbers when old locomotives were scrapped, as if the supply of numbers was limited.

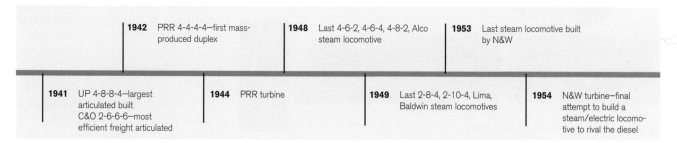

1942	PRR 4-4-4-4—first mass-produced duplex	1948	Last 4-6-2, 4-6-4, 4-8-2, Alco steam locomotive	1953	Last steam locomotive built by N&W
1941 UP 4-8-8-4—largest articulated built C&O 2-6-6-6—most efficient freight articulated		**1944** PRR turbine		**1949** Last 2-8-4, 2-10-4, Lima, Baldwin steam locomotives	**1954** N&W turbine—final attempt to build a steam/electric locomotive to rival the diesel

Model steam locomotive history and overview

By John Pryke

The first working model steam locomotives appeared in 1905, and were powered initially by wind-up (clockwork) mechanisms and then by electric motors. These early models had superstructures made of stamped and rolled steel plate with cast iron or zinc drive wheels. They ran on track made of stamped tin, which served the same function as the prototype, provided you ignored the third rail used to provide electricity to the motors and lights. Manufactured in the U.S. and the larger European countries, these models captured the overall look of contemporary steam engines, though they lacked detail, and their proportions were altered to fit around their mechanisms (see fig. 1). Leading American manufacturers Lionel, American Flyer, and Ives, and their European counterparts Hornby, Bing, and Märklin all produced catalogs for their electric train sets which were read avidly by boys (and their fathers). In England, Bassett-Lowke even made models that ran off live steam.

By 1930, many men who had grown up with toy-like electric trains began to demand engines that looked more like real trains. Small companies

Fig. 1 The Lionel 390E of 1929 was typical of early tinplate steam engines. It had many compromises in proportions and details, and its shiny paint, brass domes, and a bulb sticking out of the headlight made it look more like a toy than a prototype locomotive.

(often operating out of their basements) began to produce kits for scale model locomotives and rolling stock. Initially these models were made in O Scale ($^1\!/_{48}$ full size); but by the mid-1930s, smaller scales including OO ($^1\!/_{76}$) and HO ($^1\!/_{87}$) emerged to fit layouts in small spaces such as apartments. Initially, scale steam engines featured cast bronze or lead boilers and mechanisms made of brass and steel. The parts were rough, with the finishing and detailing left to the modeler. A machine shop was often needed to drill and tap screw holes, solder parts together, and smooth rough sand castings—still for those with the time and patience, a scale model locomotive

ultimately emerged.

In 1937, the world's largest toy train maker, Lionel, stunned the hobby by introducing an exact O Scale model of the New York Central's Hudson express passenger engine (see fig. 2). The model was made of zinc alloy die-castings that reproduced even the smallest detail, and was sold either ready-to-run or as an easy to build kit. Within a year Lionel brought out an OO scale version of its Hudson, with the same exquisite detailing as its big brother. However, the cost of tooling for die-castings was high ($75,000 for Lionel's Hudson), and smaller firms could not afford to offer new die-cast models at affordable prices. In HO, a scale growing faster than all the others combined, ingenious manufacturers produced hybrid models. Mantua combined boilers and cabs made of stamped brass with die-cast details (see fig. 3), while Varney used cast brass or lead superstructures with die-cast drivers, trucks and details.

In December 1941, World War II brought a halt to scale model railroading, as the manufacturers switched to war production (often precision instruments). With victory in 1945, these same vendors switched back to producing railroad models. Even though the war had yielded new, inexpensive materials such as plastic, the hobby industry, domi-

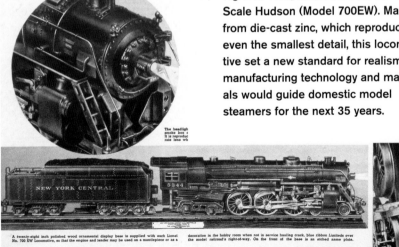

Fig. 2 In 1937, Lionel introduced its O Scale Hudson (Model 700EW). Made from die-cast zinc, which reproduced even the smallest detail, this locomotive set a new standard for realism. Its manufacturing technology and materials would guide domestic model steamers for the next 35 years.

The headlight smoke box c It is reproduc zale lens wh

NEW YORK CENTRAL 5344

A twenty-eight inch polished wood ornamental display base is supplied with each Lionel No. 700 EW Locomotive, so that the engine and tender may be used on a mantlepiece or as a decoration in the hobby room when not in service hauling track, blue ribbon Limiteds over the model railroad's right-of-way. On the front of the base is an etched name plate.

4   1975 Reproduction, Greenberg Publishing Co.

Greenberg Publishing Co.

Fig. 3 (above left) Pre-war HO steam engines, like Mantua's Reading Atlantic, combined stamped brass boilers, cabs, and tenders with die-cast chassis, drivers, and details.

Fig. 4 (above right) Introduced in early 1952, the Mantua Pacific set a new standard for HO steam engine kits. Like Lionel's pre-war O scale Hudson, it consisted primarily of well-detailed zamac castings.

Fig. 5 (left) The IMP "Mini-Roller" was one of the first crude brass imports. It lacked detail and ran badly, but its $7.50 price tag was well under U.S.-made products.

nated by small manufacturers, could not re-tool over night. One immediate change, however, was the switch from 6 to 12 volt permanent magnet motors, which gave superior performance. Therefore, until 1949, most model steam engines were basically pre-war designs, with better detailing and improved mechanisms.

Banner years for the introduction of wholly new locomotives made from detailed pressure die-castings came in 1951 and '52. Perhaps the best example was the Mantua Pacific in HO (see fig. 4). Composed entirely of highly detailed zamac (a zinc aluminum alloy) castings, this passenger steam engine was easy to assemble, performed flawlessly, and had an affordable price tag. You only needed some files, a screwdriver, a pointed center punch (for the valve gear rivets), and a

couple of evenings to assemble the kit. The range of new steam motive power in HO alone was impressive, ranging from small 0-4-0 switchers to the large Bowser 4-6-6-4 articulated.

Even as U.S. manufacturers introduced their new lines of die-cast steamers, the first brass locomotives from Japan were beginning to appear. Very inexpensive and poorly detailed, they were made from brass stampings, etchings, and turnings. These early offerings, imported by International Model Products, sold for extremely low prices. The "Min-Roller" (see fig. 5), was a typical example. Not only did it lack detail (the drivers were solid wheels with no spokes), but its running characteristics were poor and its motor unreliable. However, only five years later, a new, much higher quality family of

imported brass steam engines came on the market with a "bang" as Pacific Fast Mail announced a two truck Shay in HO (see fig. 6). Over the next 10 years, more than 100 imported brass steam engines were released, ranging in size from small industrial switchers to large articulateds. Thanks to small production runs, low-cost labor, and manual assembly, at least 15-20 imported brass engines appeared for each die-cast model made in the U.S., where manufacturers had to count on high volume to amortize costly tooling. It was not until the late 1970s that the cost of brass began to climb (and then skyrocket), making brass engines the target of collectors who put them in display cases instead of on their pikes.

In the late 1950s, model steam engines made of polystyrene plastic

Fig. 6 (top left) PFM's 1955 HO two truck Shay was the first high-quality imported brass steam locomotive on the market.

Fig. 7 (left) Rivarossi's plastic Indiana Harbor Belt 0-8-0 heavy switcher, introduced in 1960, was one of the best-detailed steam engines on the market.

Fig. 8 (above) The Bachmann Norfolk & Western J1 was an example of the plastic steam locomotives made in Hong Kong. Initially offered in HO, this N scale version appeared in 1989.

Fig. 9 (left) The Bachmann 2-8-0, announced in 1997, featured a styrene superstructure with separately applied plastic piping and fittings. This excellent detailing, plus its can motor, smooth running drive, and affordable price made this locomotive a clear alternative to the high-priced brass imports.

Model Railroader Magazine

Fig. 10 (right) Life-Like's massive Norfolk & Western Class Y-3 2-8-8-2 articulated was the largest of the new family of high-quality plastic steam locomotives.

Model Railroader Magazine

made their first appearance, initially in HO and then in N and O scales. Although plastic model steamers were common in Europe, there were none for a U.S. prototype. Therefore, it was not surprising that the first U.S. plastic models came from an Italian manufacturer, Rivarossi. Consisting of a well-detailed styrene superstructure and tender with metal and plastic chassis, these engines were priced below domestic die-cast zamac models, yet carried equivalent (or better) detail (see fig. 7). Among the initial offerings were several large articulateds, which included ingenious drives that allowed them to negotiate 18" radius curves—ideal for smaller pikes. By 1970, plastic steam engines also arrived from Hong Kong (see fig. 8). However, while foreign vendors expanded their lines of U.S. prototype models, domestic manufacturers had trouble with plastic steamers. Athearn, who had set the standard for low-cost plastic diesels, tried in vain to apply the same engineering to steam power. The three steam engines that Athearn brought to market did not compete against better designed imports, and were withdrawn in less than five years. Several U.S. manufacturers substituted plastic for zamac in their existing molds, thereby lowering the cost of their kits to a limited extent.

Between 1975 and the mid-1990s, the popularity of model steam locomotives began to wane. While the number of brass imports increased, so did the price, until these brass beauties became too expensive for the average modeler. The plastic imports sold well

to newcomers to the hobby, but their cast-on detail did not satisfy advanced modelers. The domestic manufacturers were caught in the middle, and kept trying to sell engines whose molds were made in the 1950s. Well-known manufacturers like Varney and Penn Line either went out of business or were bought up by larger firms. Model Die Casting and Mantua barely held on, and only Bowser seemed to thrive by offering superdetail parts as options with their basic kits. Like the U.S. prototype railroads, modelers converted to diesels, and the steam locomotive vanished from many pikes.

In 1997, the announcement of a new family of high-quality plastic steam locomotives changed everything. Plastic steamers had been available for forty years, but like their die cast zamac cousins, all of their details—pipes, fittings, etc—were cast as part of the boiler. Cast-on piping was only half round, not nearly as realistic as the round pieces of wire used for pipes on expensive brass imports. The Bachmann 2-8-0 (see fig. 9), featured separately cast plastic piping and details hand-applied to the boiler, as well as a smooth drive

powered by a can motor with a flywheel. The engine came fully assembled and painted in a variety of road names. It even featured a printed circuit board in the tender for the new Digital Command Control systems then coming on the market. With a price tag of $129.95 it was a clear alternative to brass imports that sold at ten times the price.

Other manufacturers, including Athearn and Life-Like, quickly followed Bachmann's lead, and the number of high-quality plastic steam engines grew. The first Life-Like "Proto2000" offering, a massive 2-8-8-2 Norfolk & Western articulated (see fig. 10), had a wealth of detail that previously could only be found on brass imports. To make this locomotive available to modelers with large and small pikes, its designers pivoted both sets of drivers so the engine could negotiate sharper curves.

Today's model steam locomotive is better than ever. Whether it be a brass import, a high-quality plastic offering, or a traditional kit, there is a steam engine that is right for virtually any layout. With new locomotives being announced every month, the age of the model steam engine is here to stay.

Model steam locomotives—current popularity and selection

By John Pryke

Today there are more model steam locomotives on the market than at any time in history. For modelers who like to build as well as run their steamers, there are kits made by long-time manufacturers including Bowser and Model Die Casting. For those who want a good-looking plastic steam engine that runs well, Rivarossi and IHC offer a wide variety of locomotives. If you are looking for a superdetailed model at an affordable price, the number of high-quality plastic steam engines continues to grow with offerings from Athearn, Bachmann, Broadway Limited, and the newer Rivarossi locomotives, to mention a few. For modelers with a larger budget there is a continuing stream of brass imports.

While the majority of these locomotives are available in HO, other scales—N, S, O, and G—are not far behind. A new age of steam is here; and for those of us who can't resist the sheer excitement inspired by a model of a mighty steam engine, it should be here for many years to come.

Here is a table showing the availability of model steam locomotives for the more popular wheel arrangements. It covers kit, plastic, high-quality plastic, and brass offerings. Since virtually every wheel arrangement has been made in brass (in many cases for several different railroads), the term "availability" can mean new, or currently not in production, but available used through brass dealers.

Selection of Model Steam Locomotives on Today's Market

Wheel Arrangement	Kits	Plastic	High-Quality Plastic	Brass (new or used)
0-4-0	X	X		X**
0-6-0	X	X	X	X**
0-8-0	X	X	X	X**
0-10-0				X**
2-6-0	X	X		X**
2-8-0	X	X	X	X**
2-10-0	X	X*	X	X**
4-4-0	X	X	X	X**
4-6-0	X	X	X	X**
2-6-2	X	X		X**
2-8-2	X	X	X	X**
2-10-2	X			X**
2-8-4	X*	X	X	X**
4-4-2	X			X**
4-6-2	X	X	X	X**
4-8-2	X	X	X	X**
4-10-2				X**
4-6-4	X*	X	X	X**
4-8-4	X	X	X	X**
0-6-6-0				X**
2-6-6-2	X*			X**
2-6-6-4			X	X**
2-6-6-6			X	X**
2-8-8-0		X		
2-8-8-2		X	X	X**
2-8-8-4				X**
4-4-4-4	X		X	X**
4-6-6-4	X	X	X	X**
4-8-8-2		X		X**
4-8-8-4	X	X	X	X**
Shay	X		X	X**
Heisler		X	X	X**
Climax	X*		X	X**

Key: *   May no longer be available
        ** Check with brass dealer(s) for what prototypes are available

Model steam locomotives—new types of construction

By John Pryke

Today's model steam engines use materials and assembly methods very different from those of the past. The die-cast kits introduced in the early 1950s consisted of zamac castings for the major components: boiler, cab, cylinders, frame, pilot, tender shell, and tender base. Drivers, pilot wheels, tender trucks, and motor were all factory assembled. The rods and valve gear were nickel-plated brass stampings that had to be screwed or riveted together. There were also a few separate details—handrail stanchions, whistle, bell, etc.—that fit into holes drilled in the boiler. Machine screws held all of the major parts together. Most kits could be assembled in a few evenings, and the most difficult work was filing off the "flash" from the parting lines between the dies.

Imported brass locomotives came ready-to-run out of the box. The only work required of the modeler was to disassemble the locomotive, paint the parts, put them back together again, and mount the couplers. Plastic steam engines were also ready-to-run, but they came factory painted and lettered in a variety of roadnames. As with the die-cast kits, the major components were held together by machine screws.

If you wanted to superdetail a locomotive to match a specific prototype, there were a large number of highly detailed brass castings on the market. These could be soldered to brass engines or glued to plastic or zamac locomotives, a task made easier by cyanoacrylate adhesive (CA) introduced in the early 1970s.

The advent of high-quality plastic steam engines introduced new materials and methods of construction. Boiler, tender, cab, and other major

Fig. 1 This photo shows the mechanism slug of a Bachmann 2-8-0. The right half of the slug above the drivers contains the motor and belt-driven worm gear. The left half of the slug is lying in the foreground.

components continued to be made of styrene. Since styrene is slightly flexible, many parts now snap in place, like the cab to the boiler. Pipes and fittings that are separately applied to the boiler are made either of wire or an engineering plastic, which is very flexible so that routine handling will not break the pipes. Detail fittings, such as valves and joints, are cast as part of the piping. Unfortunately, engineering plastic pipes cannot be cemented to styrene boilers with commercially available glues, so these parts are held in place by a tapered pin on the pipe which is force fitted into a hole in the boiler. Therefore, many separate pipes and details can be applied to these locomotives. For example, Life-Like's USRA 0-8-0 contains over 300 parts, most of them details.

Another new assembly concept is in the mechanism. Traditional zamac, brass, and plastic engines had a metal frame with slots for driver axles, and a cover plate to hold the drivers in place. The motor was usually mounted on top of the frame, and powered the drivers through a worm and gear. The new high-quality plastic engines use a cast zamac "slug," which fits inside the boiler to provide weight for traction. The slug consists of two halves (see fig. 1), which are insulated from each other. The drivers, whose axles are similarly insulated, provide pickup to the motor through each half of the slug. All of the drive components—motor, gears, and even a toothed belt in the case of Bachmann—fit within the slug. The two halves of the slug are held together by screws, and can be separated for maintenance.

DETAILING
Model Steam Locomotives

No matter how well-detailed a model steam locomotive is when you purchase it, there may be some additional parts that you would like to add. This may include making the engine look more like the steamers that ran on a railroad that you model, or creating an exact replica of a specific locomotive (railroad and road number) that you remember. If you have your own road name, you may want to add details that you think are appropriate. Luckily, there are a vast number of detail parts on the market, usually brass castings, that you can buy to add to your model.

However, why change a beautiful out-of-the-box model? Many of the model steam engines on the market today, particularly high-quality plastic engines and traditional kits, represent USRA prototypes. In 1917, when the U.S. entered World War I, the railroads were nationalized under the United States Railroad Administration (USRA). One of the USRA's first tasks was to create a set of standard locomotives and rolling stock designs to speed construction and maintenance through common, interchangeable parts. After the war was over and the railroads returned to private ownership, these designs were still manufactured, but unique modifications were made by each railroad. Over time, additional changes were made in the railroad's shops so that, by the 1940s, a copy of a USRA 2-8-2 built for the New York Central looked quite different than one built for the Union Pacific. It's up to you to add the details that will differentiate your locomotive from the standard prototype.

This section contains four articles which describe adding unique details to model locomotives. While each author tells you what to add, the more important message is *how to do it*. Attaching brass details and piping to a die-cast metal locomotive is not the same as adding the same details to an engine made of styrene. After you have read these articles, you will know how to make your model steam engine look the way you want. *John Pryke*

ONE Make a good engine great

Turn a good plastic locomotive into a masterpiece by changing a few details to match your prototype

By John Pryke
Photos by the author

The high-quality plastic steam locomotives on hobby shop shelves today are more than just ready-to-run. They offer the modeler an opportunity to modify and detail the locomotive into a layout showpiece.

A new family of HO steam locomotives has revolutionized the market over the last four years. Made of plastic with exceptional detail and ultra smooth operation, these locomotives, such as the Athearn 2-8-2 Mikado, the Bachmann Shay, and the Life-Like 2-8-8-2, have brought new life to steam modeling and are a true alternative to brass. Most of these engines represent United States Railroad Administration or other standardized designs and will be run by many modelers right "out of the box."

Yet by prying or cutting off unwanted details and replacing them with new valves, piping, and the like, you can modify these locomotives to suit your individual taste or represent a particular prototype.

But why redetail one of these excellent models? Perhaps you would like it to be a closer match to the railroad you are modeling. You may want to learn some new modeling techniques, or you may find that detailing a locomotive is fun—as I have over the last 50 years.

I needed another 0-8-0 to switch passenger cars at the Providence station on my HO New York, New Haven & Hartford layout. Since the New Haven's first Class Y-3s, built in 1920, were USRA copies with some unique detailing, Life-Like's Proto 2000 0-8-0 made a good starting point.

After buying one and taking it out of the box, I discovered my new

The author's model New Haven Y-3 0-8-0: a superdetailed Proto 2000 USRA 0-8-0.

J.W. Swanberg Collection

Fig. 1 THE PROTOTYPE. A photo of a New Haven Y-3 taken during the late 1930s appeared in the book *New Haven Power*.

engine was made of a number of "exotic" materials with which I had little or no experience. What a great opportunity to broaden my modeling skills!

In addition, I've always enjoyed building locomotives, but over the last ten years have concentrated on finishing my layout and implementing more prototypical operations. So detailing the new 0-8-0 to match my

other Y-3s was also a chance to have some fun and take a break from building scenery and developing a freight car waybill system.

Whatever your reason, these new steam locomotives use a variety of materials and assembly techniques which are quite different from those used on metal kits such as Bowser or Roundhouse.

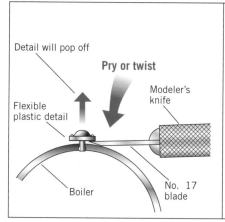

Fig. 2 CHISEL. Insert a modeler's knife with a no. 17 chisel blade under a piece of detail to pry it free of the boiler or slice it off.

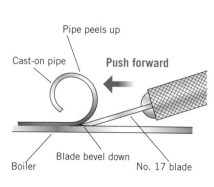

Fig. 3 REMOVING CAST-ON PIPING. Cast-on piping can be removed from the boiler with a no. 17 chisel blade, beveled side down.

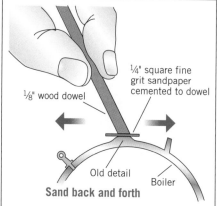

Fig. 4 TIGHT FIT. You can make a small sanding tool from a wooden dowel with sandpaper glued to its angled edge.

Plan your project

The first step in detailing a locomotive for a specific railroad is to obtain plans and photos of the prototype. These should include right, left, and three-quarter views.

I found several photos (see fig. 1) of Y-3s in the book *New Haven Power*. Plans of the original USRA locomotive are in the *Model Railroader Cyclopedia: Vol. 1 Steam Locomotives*.

Like many other roads, the New Haven Railroad ordered its USRA 0-8-0 copies with fittings and piping that matched its own locomotive standards. The changes included lifting injectors, vertical check valves, headlight, backup light, Vulcan tender trucks, and some unique piping, all of which gave these Y-3s a distinctive look. These details dictated the changes I made to the Proto 2000 model.

I studied the photos and plan, then made a list of the model's details I needed to remove and the new parts I had to add. A wide selection of HO steam locomotive detail parts are available from several manufacturers. After looking through some catalogs, I found the parts I needed.

Know your plastic

Before removing or adding details, you need to understand the materials used to manufacture this new family of engines. Major superstructure compo-

nents (boiler, cab, tender shell, etc.) are made of styrene. Details above the running gear are either separately applied or molded as part of the boiler shell.

Depending on the manufacturer, the separate parts can be made of styrene, wire, or a slippery engineering plastic chosen for its flexibility.

Piping and components below the running boards are made of the same flexible plastic so they will not break when the locomotive is handled.

The chassis usually consists of two cast-metal halves that hold the motor and drive train in place and provide weight for traction. The side rods and valve gear are cast or stamped nickel silver, which may be chemically blackened by the manufacturer.

Disassemble and explore

I start my detailing projects by disassembling the model into its major components: boiler, cab, chassis (drivers, drive train, motor, etc.), tender shell, tender underframe, and trucks (leading, trailing, and tender).

Manufacturer-supplied instructions may or may not explain the disassembly process clearly, so here are some hints to follow.

Remove the engine's leading and trailing trucks. Then look for screws at the rear of the chassis, which may also hold the drawbar in place, or screws centered under the cylinders. Remove each screw individually, and if the

chassis loosens, that screw holds the locomotive's components together.

Pull the boiler upward and rotate the rear of the chassis downward until it clears the boiler. Slide the boiler forward off the chassis. Do not force the parts as there may be a holding screw you haven't noticed.

Remove the cab if you need to repaint the window frames or front doors. Some manufacturers' cabs are screwed in place and easily taken off. Others are held in place by tabs (as in the case of the Proto 2000 0-8-0). These may be removed by inserting a small blade under the edge of the cab near its front corner and gently prying out and up. Don't apply too much pressure or you will break the cab.

Look at the bottom of the tender for a single screw on the center line and tabs at the rear. Alternately, there may be screws at each corner. Remove these and either lift the shell off or hinge it upward off the tabs. Do not unscrew the tender trucks as a first step; they may be held on with nuts accessible only with the shell removed.

Out with the old details

The next step is to remove any unwanted details separately applied at the factory. If the part is made of a flexible plastic, it is usually held in place by a pin on the part force-fitted into a hole in the boiler. I insert a

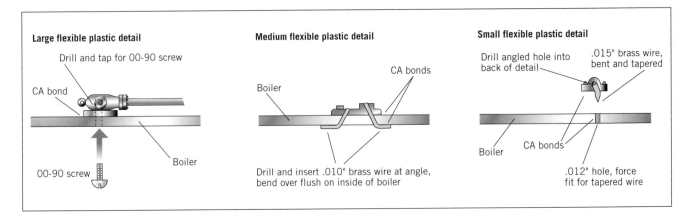

Large flexible plastic detail

Drill and tap for 00-90 screw

CA bond

00-90 screw

Boiler

Medium flexible plastic detail

Boiler

CA bonds

Drill and insert .010" brass wire at angle, bend over flush on inside of boiler

Small flexible plastic detail

Drill angled hole into back of detail

.015" brass wire, bent and tapered

Boiler

CA bonds

.012" hole, force fit for tapered wire

Fig. 5 (above) MECHANICAL JOINTS. Here are several different methods for mechanically joining a detail made of flexible plastic to a styrene shell or metal surface. The size and location of the detail determines the method. John suggests that wherever possible these details should be secured from inside the boiler.

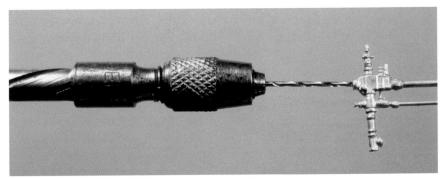

Fig. 6 PIPE HOLE. Using a pin vise and a bit .002"-.003" larger than the pipe, John drills a hole for a pipe ½₂" deep in a lifting injector casting.

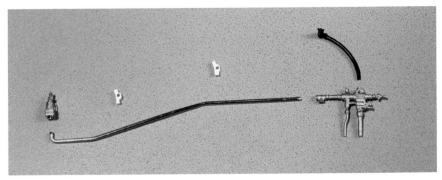

Fig. 7 INJECTOR SYSTEM. These are the parts for the new injector system. From left to right they include: a vertical check valve (brass casting), injector pipe (brass wire), two pipe supports (styrene), lifting injector (brass casting), and turret pipe (black flexible plastic).

Manufacturers of detail parts for HO steam locomotives

Bowser Mfg. Co., Inc.
1302 Jordan Ave.
Montoursville, PA 17754
Catalog price: $14.

Precision Scale Co., Inc.
P. O. Box 278
3961 Highway 93 North
Stevensville, MT 59870
HO/HOn3 steam locomotive catalog price: $18.

Cary Locomotive Works
Parts listed in the Bowser catalog

Cal-Scale
Parts listed in the Bowser and Walthers catalogs

Custom Finishing
379 Tully Rd.
Orange, MA 01364
Parts listed in the Walthers catalog or send SSAE (11" x 12", 97 cents postage) for parts list.
Specify HO or O.

modeler's knife with a no. 17 chisel blade between the part and boiler, and gently pry upward (see fig. 2). The pin will lift out without damaging the detail or boiler.

If the part is made of styrene or metal, it is bonded to the boiler either with cyanoacrylate adhesive (CA) or styrene cement. I first apply a CA debonder to the inside of the boiler shell where the part comes through or to the outside where the part is attached. If the detail does not loosen, then plastic cement was used

to bond and it must be cut off. I use a knife with a very sharp blade to slice off the part as cleanly as possible.

Finally, I remove any unwanted piping or details that may be cast onto the boiler. I use a modeler's knife with a no. 17 blade and keep the blade's beveled side next to the boiler. This lets me hold the knife at an angle while the blade's edge is parallel to the boiler surface. I gently move the knife along the pipe, allowing the unwanted plastic to curl up over the blade (see fig. 3). It may take

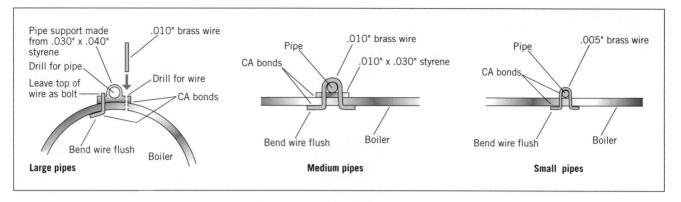

Large pipes	Medium pipes	Small pipes

Fig. 8 (above) PIPE SUPPORTS. Pipe supports are an authentic, effective way to secure brass or flexible plastic pipes to a boiler. Three types are shown.

Fig. 9 (right) NEW PARTS IN PLACE. The new injector is shown after installation on the boiler. The brass pipes below the running board were installed later and secured to the firebox with pipe supports. A piece of .015" brass, secured with CA, was used as a bracket to hold the inlet pipe under the cab floor.

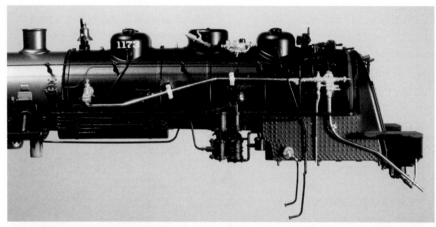

Effectiveness of bonding mechanisms on different materials

	Styrene	Flexible plastic	Zinc casting	Brass	Remarks
CA	Good	Poor	Good	Good	Notes 1, 2
Plastic cement	Excellent	Bad	Bad	Bad	Note 3
Epoxy	Good	Marginal	Good	Good	Note 4
PlioBond, Goo	Bad	Good	Marginal	Marginal	Note 5
Mechanical	Good	Good	Good	Good	Note 6

1. Use gap-filling adhesive for best results.
2. Flexible acetal plastic must be roughened with a file if CA is to work.
3. Fast acting cement (Tenax 7R) has least effect on surface finish.
4. Messy to use. Leaves thick, visible bond, even when painted.
5. May craze surface of styrene and ABS. Joints remain flexible, do not harden.
6. See fig. 5 for examples.

several passes to remove the pipe.

When I have removed all unwanted detail, I fill in any holes with modeler's putty, or a piece of .010" styrene if a hole is large. I then sand the putty, the edges of styrene patches, and any humps where piping has been removed. I use fine sandpaper, 220 grit for rough sanding and 600 grit for a final finish. Where it is difficult to reach the area, I cut a piece of ⅛"-diameter dowel 6" long, with one end beveled at a 30-degree angle, and glue a small (¼" square) piece of sandpaper to this end. This lets me work in tight spaces (see fig. 4). Take your time when sanding. Try to hide all scars so the boiler will appear as if the detail you've removed never existed.

Making bonds strong

A key factor in adding new details is knowing how to attach parts made from different materials. Mechanical bonds are often best for securing engineering plastics to styrene or metal. Figure 5 shows some examples.

Wherever possible, I like to secure a detail from the inside of the boiler. If the new detail has a casting sprue or pin on its backside, I drill a hole in the boiler, pass the pin through, and secure it from the inside with gap-filling CA. This keeps the glue off the surface of the boiler. Where pipes join fittings, I drill a hole in the fit-

ting, insert the pipe, and cement it with CA.

As an example of these techniques, let's look at replacing the injector, check valve, and associated piping on my Proto 2000 0-8-0 to match the NH Y-3. After removing the existing parts from the boiler, I marked the location of each new detail (lifting

Fig. 10 SANDER. John uses a dowel covered with sandpaper to create a slot for a feedwater heater tank.

Fig. 11 FEEDWATER HEATER. The embedded feedwater heater casting is neatly glued to the top of the smokebox.

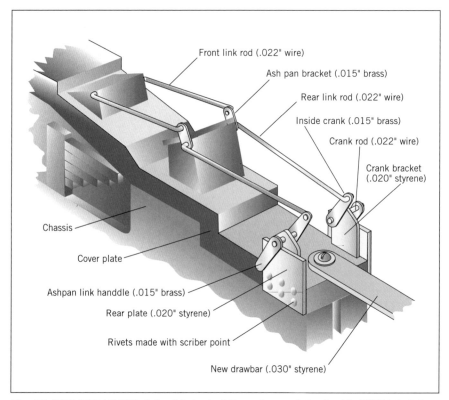

Front link rod (.022" wire)
Ash pan bracket (.015" brass)
Rear link rod (.022" wire)
Inside crank (.015" brass)
Crank rod (.022" wire)
Crank bracket (.020" styrene)
Chassis
Cover plate
Ashpan link handdle (.015" brass)
Rear plate (.020" styrene)
Rivets made with scriber point
New drawbar (.030" styrene)

Fig. 12 ASH PAN LINKS. John fabricated the ash pan links for his USRA 0-8-0.

injector, check valve, pipe holders) with a fine pencil. I then drilled holes in the injector casting (see fig. 6) and check valve for the connecting pipes. Gluing the pipes in these holes creates a strong joint.

I cut all of the parts to exact size and test-fitted them before final installation (see fig. 7). I also made two pipe supports from .030" x .040" styrene to hold the feed pipe—different types of pipe supports are shown in fig. 8.

After gluing the check valve in place, I slid the supports onto the water feed pipe and fitted it into the valve on one end and the injector on the other. I put a little gap-filling CA on the back of the injector and held it in place on the boiler while the cement set. I cut the existing flexible plastic turret pipe to fit, inserted one end in the top of the injector and reattached the other end to the turret. Finally, I put a drop of gap-filling CA onto all joints. Figure 9 shows the new injector system.

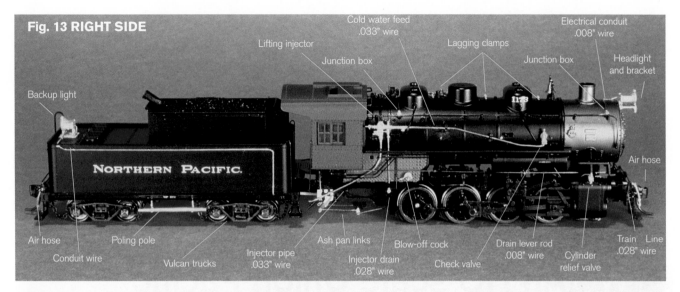

Fig. 13 RIGHT SIDE

Backup light — Lifting injector — Junction box — Cold water feed .033" wire — Lagging clamps — Junction box — Electrical conduit .008" wire — Headlight and bracket — Air hose

Air hose — Conduit wire — Poling pole — Vulcan trucks — Injector pipe .033" wire — Ash pan links — Injector drain .028" wire — Blow-off cock — Check valve — Drain lever rod .008" wire — Cylinder relief valve — Train Line .028" wire

Fig. 14 LEFT SIDE

Pipe support styrene — Cold water feed .033" wire — Whistle — Barco low water alarm — Lifting injector

Train line to air hose .028" wire — Cylinder relief valve — Check valve — Blowoff cock — Injector drain .028" wire — Injector feed .033" wire — Rerail frogs

Embedding parts

While not needed on my 0-8-0, you may encounter parts that must be partially embedded in the boilers of other locomotives. An Elesco feedwater heater tank mounted in the top of the smokebox is an example.

To ensure the tank will fit snugly into the boiler, I make a tool from a piece of dowel, the same diameter as the tank, with a small piece of sandpaper glued around it.

I carefully sand the boiler, making sure the slot the sanding creates remains horizontal (see fig. 10). After the slot is sanded deep enough, I cement the brass feedwater tank in place with CA (see fig. 11).

Similar techniques can be used for front-end throttle covers and other embedded parts.

Making do by making your own

Unfortunately, not all the details you will need are available, and you may have to fabricate some parts from scratch. An example on my 0-8-0 was the lack of ash pan door links under the firebox. Although very visible on the prototype, they would have interfered with the model's wide drawbar, which carries wires for DCC to the tender.

I don't use DCC and had rewired the engine to run without a tender. Therefore, I made a new, narrow drawbar from .030" styrene leaving room for the links. Since no suitable parts were available, I fabricated the linkage components from .020" styrene and .022" brass wire (see fig. 12). I punched the six rivets in the

end plate with the point of a scriber.

The finished links installed on my Y-3 can be seen in the side views of the locomotive. These links are good examples of simple parts you can make yourself that will add to the appearance of your model.

Figures 13 and 14 show the right and left sides of my New Haven Y-3 prior to painting, with the new parts labeled as a guide for similar detailing projects.

Painting and finishing

Prior to painting the model, I disassembled it into the major components. I used masking tape across the open back of the cab and under the open roof hatches to protect the green cab interior. I also cut pieces of tape to protect the cab windows. I spray-painted the locomotive with

Polly Scale acrylic paint, using Grimy Black for the base coat.

I hooked clip leads to each half of the chassis and spun the drivers while painting them to prevent any shadowing behind the rods and valve gear. I used MOW Gray on the smokebox and firebox. Milwaukee Road Gray served as drip marks from the pop valves and other "leaky" fittings.

I gave the joint between the tender deck and sides, plus the water hatch, a light coat of Rust, while the trucks and running gear (with the drivers spinning) received a light spray of Earth.

I cleaned any stray paint off the wheel treads using twisted-up tissue dipped in Polly Scale Easy-Lift-Off paint remover. I turned the tissue point frequently to prevent the removed paint from returning to the wheel tread. I polished each tread by gently holding a soft eraser against its surface.

After reassembly, I applied the road name and number with dry transfers. I applied touches of rust to fittings, truck springs, and coupler faces by hand using a 3/0 brush. Where the weathering and lettering colors were too intense, I applied a very light spray of Grimy Black to tone them down. I then glued MV lenses to the headlight and backup light.

Finally, I cleaned the wheels using thinner and placed the Y-3 in service on my layout. It took longer to bring this locomotive into service, but I can run it now with pride for taking the time to go beyond the box.

TWO An HO scale Union Pacific
Railroad-specific details for Athearn's Light Mike

By Steve Orth
Photos by the author

When Athearn released its HO model of the USRA Light 2-8-2, it quickly got my attention, as I model the Union Pacific of the late 1950s. Since UP rostered 20 USRA Light Mikes, I knew this locomotive would make a nice addition to my lineup.

Lots of photos and prototype information on the UP's USRA Mikes can be found in the Vol. 1, no. 4 issue of *The Streamliner*, published by the Union Pacific Historical Society. Additional details can be found in *Motive Power of the Union Pacific* by Kratville and Rank.

The *Streamliner* article included photos of both sides of UP 2498, taken in 1947 and '49. With these photos, the Athearn model, and parts catalogs in hand, I set out to detail the Light Mike to match a specific UP prototype.

Background

The United States Railroad Administration was established during World War I in response to delays in the movement of needed supplies. One of the main causes of these delays was a shortage of motive power. The USRA's solution was a series of standard steam locomotive

Athearn's USRA Light Mikado offers HO modelers tremendous kitbashing and detailing possibilities. Steve Orth shows how some minor modifications can result in a detailed model of the Union Pacific prototype.

designs. A total of 12 designs, including a light 2-8-2, were developed by 1918.

Union Pacific was one of the railroads that received USRA Light Mikes. A total of 40 engines were delivered to the UP system, 20 to the UP (nos. 2295- 2314, later renumbered 2480-2499) and 20 to subsidiary Oregon Short Line (nos. 2535-2554). Since they were larger than the 2-8-2s already on the locomotive roster, the UP called its USRA Light Mikados heavy Mikes, class "MK Special."

Many modifications were made to these engines over the years. The most obvious occurred in the 1930s when gigantic Sweeney smokestacks replaced the original ones. Other modifications included wider footboards on the pilot, modifications to the sanding lines, and rerouted cold water feed piping. The tenders retained their as-built appearance, although some engines received

Vanderbilt tenders in later years.

These locomotives, classified "MK Special" by the UP, served for many years, with most lasting into the early 1950s. The last MK Special was retired in December 1959.

Disassembly

Although the Mike is a difficult model to disassemble, I arrived at the following method. I began by sliding the cab upward, releasing it from the boiler and running boards. Next I removed the smokebox front and disconnected the headlight.

After taking off the lead and trailing trucks, I removed the screw through the steam chest. Then I disengaged the tabs on the rear of the boiler, pulled up on the rear of the boiler until it cleared the motor, and slid the boiler forward until it released from the running boards. Although I was concerned that something would break, the boiler finally released and was set aside.

Last, I removed the four screws that hold the weight and motor to the chassis, two on the front above the steam chest and two on the rear at the base of the weight. Removing the motor and weight completed the disassembly.

Boiler modifications

I began by removing the stack and filing off the stack base. The air pump steam line from the turret was no longer present on my prototype, so I carved it off, covering the surrounding details with masking tape to avoid damaging them during the process.

Then I carefully removed mold parting lines from the tops of the smokebox, sand dome, and steam dome (not the boiler, as that line represents the seam between the lagging sheets). Using a motor tool, I carefully cut the cold water feed lines off both sides of the boiler. Then all areas affected by this plastic surgery were sanded and polished until smooth.

Study prototype photos before proceeding, as some of the UP 2-8-2s retained the as-delivered sand pipes. My prototype didn't, so I removed

Union Pacific Mikado 2495 double-heads with a Big Boy near Granite Canyon on Sherman Hill in Wyoming.

Lucius Beebe

Steve's painted and lettered model leaves town with a long freight in tow.

the Athearn sand pipes and valves, saving the valves for reuse. I removed the grabs from the sand dome, fabricating new ones from .012" wire. Then I secured the stack with epoxy.

While the epoxy was setting, I removed the headlight from the smokebox front. As I cut the headlight housing off the bracket, I was careful not to damage the bracket or the cylinder which holds the headlight assembly in place on the smokebox. Then I drilled out the back of the Precision Scale headlight casting with a no. 54 drill to accommodate a bulb and wiring. Next I epoxied the headlight casting to the bracket and put this assembly aside until after painting.

The train indicator boards are from

Cal-Scale. To mount them, I drilled a no. 54 hole on the stack's transverse centerline, approximately .12" from the stack base, and inserted the stud from the bottom of the indicator board. Do not glue in place until after painting.

I replaced the turbo-generator with a more detailed Precision Scale part. After removing the plastic generator I filled the mounting hole with styrene. Then I drilled two no. 64 holes and used cyanoacrylate adhesive (CA) to hold the new generator securely in place.

I cut a piece of .010" x .030" styrene strip ⅛" long. After drilling a no. 79 hole in one end, I added it to the power control reverse lever, extending it above the running

21

board. Once the model was reassembled, I inserted one end of a piece of .012" wire in the previously drilled hole. I ran the other end of the wire through a hole in the front wall of the cab (see photos on page 23).

Piping installation

The first piping I added was the cold water feed pipes. I kept the original fittings but added .040" wire, bent at a 90-degree angle. The pipes run from the fittings toward the bottom of the boiler, ending where the pipes go through the running boards.

I secured the previously removed sanding valves to the base of the sand dome with liquid cement. Then I bent new sand lines from .019" wire, attaching them to the boiler with CA.

After forming a new steam line from .019" wire, I ran it from the turret to the running board. I drilled two no. 70 holes, one in the top of the smokebox and the second in the side of the smokebox. I bent a piece of .028" wire and inserted it in the top hole, gluing the loop from an Athearn diesel stanchion (to simulate the prototype clamp) in the second hole before running the wire through the "clamp."

Turning to the running board/firebox area, I added a length of .040" wire to the firebox sides as seen in the photos. A short length of .019" wire, simulating the exhaust line from the stoker, was added to the firebox on the fireman's side. Finally, I added a short length of .028" brass wire from the air compressor to the injector.

Pilot modifications

The UP 2-8-2s had the footboards on their pilots widened. A study of the photos reveals that the shops apparently removed the four outermost vertical bars on the pilot, installing wide footboards in their place. I modified my model the same way.

I started by using flush-cutting nippers to remove the outer four bars on each side of the pilot, the angled protrusion on the outside pilot support, and the small footboards and brackets.

Then I bent four new footboard brackets from $\frac{1}{64}$" x $\frac{1}{16}$" brass bar (see fig. 1). To mount the brackets, I drilled two no. 77 holes in each bracket and inserted brass nut-bolt-washer castings. I held the brackets

in position and marked the location of the holes on the pilot. After drilling through the pilot, I inserted the n.b.w. castings, bent the pins, and added a drop of CA to hold the brackets in place.

The footboards are from Detail Associates. After I trimmed the boards to fit on each side, I split a third board horizontally and used it for the short vertical board on the back of the footboard. I cut two strips of .010" x .080" styrene, .33" long, and fastened them to the back side of the brackets with CA.

I cut the flag holders from the corners of the pilots and drilled no. 79 holes in their place. Then I made a grab iron from .012" wire and glued it in place.

Cab details

Feeling the plastic grab irons were too thick, I removed them, filled the holes with .025" styrene rod cut flush, and fabricated new grabs from .012" wire. I also made new grab irons for the cab roof. A Detail Associates wire eyelet secures the corner of the L-shaped roof grab and I added n.b.w. castings to the end of both roof grabs.

The final items installed were the Athearn handrails and stanchions. I needed to drill an extra no. 72 hole just behind the relocated sand valves for one of the stanchions.

Tender

I started work on the tender by removing all the plastic grab irons, and filling the holes with .025" styrene rod which I cemented in place and cut flush once dry. After removing the rerail frogs, I filed off the mounting lugs, taking care to preserve the I-beam shape of the frame in the process. While working on the floor, I drilled no. 79 holes in the brake lever and installed .012" wire between there and the bolsters to simulate brake rigging.

Next I epoxied the brass toolbox to the left side. Then I fashioned grab irons from .012" wire, securing them with CA.

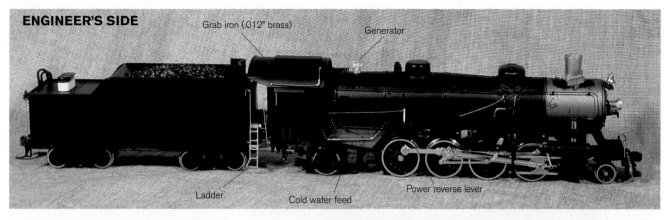

ENGINEER'S SIDE
Grab iron (.012" brass)
Generator
Ladder
Cold water feed
Power reverse lever

FIREMAN'S SIDE
Number boards
Stack
Water hatch (extended)
.015" wire
.012" wire
Toolbox

After removing the front stirrup and upper steps, I filed the affected areas smooth. Then I extended the front platform with .040" x .060" styrene. The new front ladders are attached to the tender deck and frame with epoxy.

I raised the height of the water hatch with a piece of .015" styrene. After gluing the styrene to the hatch, I filed and sanded the assembly smooth. Then I replaced the molded grab irons with .012" wire and cemented the hatch in place. Installation of the ladder and marker lights completed the tender.

Painting and weathering

With the detailing work complete, I was ready to paint my model. I started by masking off the firebox. Then I sprayed the model Floquil Engine Black, lightened by adding one part Reefer White to nine parts black.

Since none of the prototype locomotives had polished rods or wheel tires, I painted these parts of the model black also. To avoid the need

to disassemble the running gear, I painted these parts in place.

Immediately after painting, I used a brush dipped in thinner to clean the wheel surfaces, crosshead guides, and piston rods. Once the black dried, I sprayed Glosscote on any surfaces that would be decaled.

After painting the cab interior Floquil Coach Green, I masked off the boiler and painted the smokebox Scalecoat II Graphite and Oil.

I decaled the locomotive with Microscale 87-63 decals. Numerals for the indicators came from Microscale 87-36. Once the decals dried, I sealed the model with a mix of one part Dullcote and one part Glosscote.

When reassembling the locomotive, I replaced the LED with a 1.5V, 1.2 mm-diameter bulb. This required replacing the resistor on the printed-circuit board with one rated 681 ohm, ¼W. I soldered the bulb to the connector pins and ran it through the headlight.

The model was lightly drybrushed with gray to highlight the details

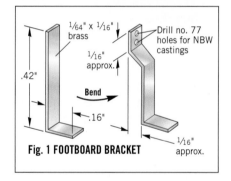

1/64" x 1/16" brass
1/16" approx.
.42"
Bend
.16"
Drill no. 77 holes for NBW castings
1/16" approx.

Fig. 1 FOOTBOARD BRACKET

and then weathered using an airbrush. I applied heavily diluted Floquil Grime, Engine Black, and Reefer White.

The Athearn plastic headlight lens fit the PSC housing perfectly. I also covered the headlight wing boards with acetate so they would be illuminated, although I haven't been able to locate the correct numbers for the boards. After I drilled out the classification and marker light housings, I added MV Product lenses.

Once I installed a Digital Command Control decoder in the tender, my detailed MK Special was ready for service, moving trains along the line as Extra 2498.

THREE A Central Vermont 2-8-0 in HO Scale

Converting Bachmann's HO scale Baldwin into a New England Alco

By Iain Rice
Model photos by Bill Zuback

The HO Bachmann Baldwin 2-8-0 is a first—a ready-to-run plastic steam locomotive approaching the quality of the better diesel models. While it's based to a large degree on an Illinois Central locomotive, the Bachmann model is a generic steamer that can be made to look a great deal like almost any medium-sized 2-8-0. One of the prototypes close to the Bachmann model is Central Vermont's N-5a class Consolidation.

Laying the model on an HO print of the Alco N-5a drawing confirmed the overall length, boiler length, diameter, and taper are all very close, or "spot on." After checking the overall dimensions, I placed the scale drawings aside and relied on prototype photographs to detail the model.

Admittedly, the wheelbase of the Bachmann engine is a little long and the cylinders are a fraction undersized. There are also other minor compromises. All these are easy to live with—especially as the goal was a

D. Nelson

Central Vermont no. 472 awaits one of her last assignments in St. Albans, Vt., in March 1957. She, and all remaining CV steam locomotives, will be retired within a week.

fleet locomotive for an operating layout and the only alternatives are rare and pricey brass imports.

The prototype

The American Locomotive Co. built a total of 16 N-5a class 2-8-0s for the Central Vermont. Numbered 460-475 and delivered in 1923, they became the workhorses of the fleet until replaced by diesels in March 1957. While sharing an identical boiler with the CV's 57"-drivered M-3a class and the P-1a class 0-8-0s, the N-5a's had 63" drivers and steam heat lines. Their 55-mph speed rating meant they could pinch-hit on passenger trains if needed.

The CV 2-8-0s saw a number of rebuildings and modifications over the years. Locomotives were equipped with feedwater heaters (Worthington or Elesco steam injectors), larger smokebox doors, and blowdown muf-

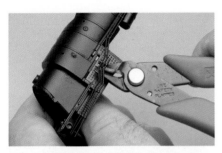

Fig. 1 REMOVING PIPES. Use flush-cutting nippers to remove the plastic pipes from the boiler. Leave the mounting pins in place.

Fig. 2 UNSTICKING DOMES. Apply some CA debonder to the inside of the domes and stack and let it sit for a few minutes.

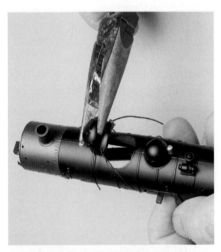

Fig. 3 REMOVING DOMES. Then use pliers to grasp the domes. They should easily lift right off the boiler.

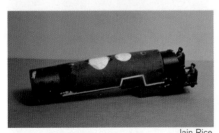

Iain Rice

Fig. 4 STRIPPED BOILER.
The only details that Iain left on the boiler are the smoke-box rivets.

flers. In earlier years, a select number of locomotives (nos. 460, 463-465, and 473) also received Bethlehem tender boosters.

Stripping a Bachmann Baldwin

The first task is to disassemble the locomotive and remove the inappropriate details. Remove the lead truck and drawbar, then loosen the screws holding the body to the chassis. Carefully pull the chassis down and away from the cast block holding the motor, belt drive, and worm gear.

The cast-metal block containing the motor and drive releases from the shell by dropping the rear end beneath the cab, then pulling gently back and down to free the smokebox end. Remove the drive system and lay it aside.

The cab is held in place with a screw inside the cab roof and two retaining clips. Remove the screw and pop the clips out of the holes.

Once the cab was off, I eased a knife between the running boards and boiler, cut the locating lugs, and popped out the running boards.

I used flush-cutting nippers (see fig. 1) to remove most of the boiler detail. I did need to use a razor saw to remove the smokebox front. For the domes and stack, I applied a small amount of cyanoacrylate adhesive (CA) debonder to the inside of the boiler (see fig. 2) and waited a few minutes before lifting these parts off with pliers (see fig. 3). I then carved away the Baldwin builder's plates and sanded the area smooth.

Filling in the gaps

The next step is to fill the grooves, slots, and holes in the boiler. The domes left the biggest holes, so I started with them. I wrapped a piece of .060" styrene around the outside of the boiler and scribed the outline of the holes onto the styrene from the inside. Then I taped the styrene to a broom handle and immersed it in very hot water. After it cooled, the styrene held its shape.

After cutting the two patches out slightly oversized, I sanded them until they fit snugly into the holes. I used some .010" styrene inside the boiler to back the patches and glued them in place. The styrene sat slightly higher than the boiler, making it easy to sand the patches until they were flush with the surrounding area.

Cutting the smaller parts from the boiler left small stubs of the mounting pins remaining. Leaving these in place as fillers, I sanded them until the surface was flush. To fill the holes without mounting pins, I used bits of plastic as plugs, cementing them in place and allowing them to dry completely before sanding flush.

I left the two rear and the front handrail stanchion holes alone, although I did fill the two holes located toward the rear of the smoke-box with body putty.

Then I used .040"-square styrene to fill the old running-board grooves. The prototype locomotives have lower running boards, making these patched areas very visible and worth the extra effort to produce a smooth finish. To prevent having a visible gap in the smokebox bottom, I removed the curved piece of the fireman's side running board and cemented it in place.

With the boiler stripped, plugged, and sanded, I used a mill file to carefully remove and smooth out the excess filler, stanchions, plugs, and other patches. I used a finer mill file, followed with successive passes of 180-, 240-, and 400-grit wet-and-dry sandpaper to achieve a smooth surface. At this stage the only Bachmann details still on the boiler were the smokebox rivets (see fig. 4).

Chassis modifications

I started the chassis modifications by fitting new steam pipes to the cylinders. I first used a jeweler's saw to remove the steam pipes and flanges on the smokebox end from the cylinder block, making sure I did not damage the lubricator fittings on top of the cylinders.

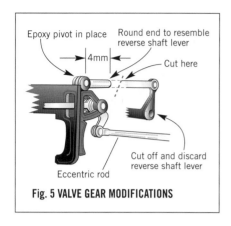

Fig. 5 VALVE GEAR MODIFICATIONS

Epoxy pivot in place
Round end to resemble reverse shaft lever
4mm
Cut here
Cut off and discard reverse shaft lever
Eccentric rod

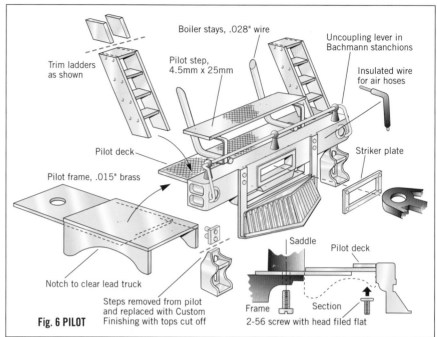

Fig. 6 PILOT

Boiler stays, .028" wire
Uncoupling lever in Bachmann stanchions
Insulated wire for air hoses
Pilot step, 4.5mm x 25mm
Trim ladders as shown
Striker plate
Pilot deck
Pilot frame, .015" brass
Notch to clear lead truck
Steps removed from pilot and replaced with Custom Finishing with tops cut off
Saddle
Pilot deck
Frame
Section
2-56 screw with head filed flat

Next I made new steam pipes from $^3/_{16}$" plastic tubing. After mounting the cylinders to the boiler, I cut pieces of tubing to length. To achieve a tight fit between the upper end of the pipes and the smokebox, I wrapped a dowel with 180-grit sandpaper and sanded the ends of the pipe to match the curve and angle of the smokebox sides.

After trimming the lower ends of the pipe until they sat neatly on top of the cylinders, I cemented the pipes in place and set the assembly aside to dry.

At this point I made some minor modifications to the Bachmann valve gear (see fig. 5). I trimmed the stamped

J.W. Swanberg

A number of the boiler and smokebox fittings are visible in this shot of N-5a no. 470.

Fig. 7 FIREMAN'S SIDE (PROTOTYPE). Note no. 470's large ashpan and the Elesco steam injector below the cab.

metal linkages until they extended $^1/_4$" behind the triangular motion bracket on both sides of the locomotive.

The shortened rods end up in the correct position to represent reverse shaft levers, although the valve rods needed to be reattached with epoxy. Then I used Xuron shears to

remove the Bachmann reverse shaft levers and molded plastic weight shaft cranks.

Modifying the stock Baker valve gear this way captures the look of the prototype Walscherts valve gear without requiring a complex conversion.

Pilot

I built a new pilot from commercial castings and brass stock. For assembly, I used high-strength, low-melt solder sold for etched brass kit assembly in Great Britain. This solder is available in the United States from International Hobbies (10556 Combrie Rd.,

J. W. Swanberg

Suite 6327, Auburn, CA 95602).

The solder I used for this project has a melting temperature of 145 degrees, although a 180-degree version is also available. A 25-watt soldering iron is sufficient for this work.

I used pieces of wet tissue to wipe away the flux residue, and as heat sinks to prevent accidentally unsoldering parts. Figure 6 shows the various components of the new pilot. After I removed the Bachmann pilot from the chassis, I made a frame extension from two layers of .015" brass. The double layer keeps the pilot the correct height above the rails.

I modified the brass Precision Scale pilot slightly. After enlarging the coupler opening, I removed the cast steps and deepened the recess behind the coupler mount to clear the pilot deck and accommodate the frame extension. Then I drilled no. 65 holes for the uncoupling lever stanchions, soldered the beam to the frame extension, and fitted the side pieces in place.

I held the coupler in place and marked the location of the mounting hole. Then, after filing the head of a short 2-56 screw flat, I soldered it to the underside of the frame extension to provide a pivot point for the coupler.

I cut the pilot deck from the Precision Scale brass safety tread and soldered it behind the beam on top of the frame extension. Next I added the ladders, using some Handi-tack to hold them in position as I soldered them to the pilot assembly.

The prototype had a raised step above the pilot deck. I cut this out of diamond-tread stock and mounted it to brackets fashioned from .015" x .030" flat brass wire. After centering this assembly on the pilot deck between the ladders, I soldered it in place.

The new pilot steps were then soldered in place beneath the pilot beam. The striker plate is .015" brass sheet cut to shape and embossed with bolt-head detail. Then I added the

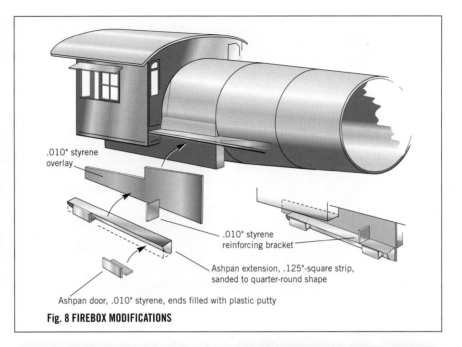

.010" styrene overlay

.010" styrene reinforcing bracket

Ashpan extension, .125"-square strip, sanded to quarter-round shape

Ashpan door, .010" styrene, ends filled with plastic putty

Fig. 8 FIREBOX MODIFICATIONS

Bill of materials

Bachmann
Spectrum 2-8-0, any road

Cal-Scale
207 headlight
210 headlight (backup light)
223 blowdown muffler
243 smokebox front
247 pop valves
251 Nathan top feed check valve
258 headlight bracket
280 marker lights
293 Nathan injector starter valves
381 cab roof hatch

Custom Finishing
115 pilot steps
155 footboard ladders

Detail Associates
2505 .015" brass wire
2506 .019" brass wire
2509 .033" brass wire
2510 .040" brass wire
2524 .015" x .030" flat brass strip

Evergreen styrene
142 .040" square strip
146 .125" square strip
9002 sheet assortment

Microscale decals
87-1027 Central Vermont
steam locomotives

Miniatures by Eric
CN triangular number box

Polly Scale
414110 Steam Power Black
414137 Grimy Black
414143 ATSF Silver
414233 BAR Gray
414281 Boxcar Red
414311 Earth

Plastruct styrene
90605 3/16" tubing
90711 .010" x .030" strip
90740 .040" square strip

Precision Scale
371 handrail stanchions
3100 whistle
31058 air reservoir
31065 bell
31136 builder's plates (Alco)
31244 steam dome
31343 tender water hatch
31454 stack base
31581 air compressor
3173 power reverse
3208 boiler steps
3335 exhaust steam injector
3430 pilot
48201 washout plugs
48254 diamond tread brass sheet

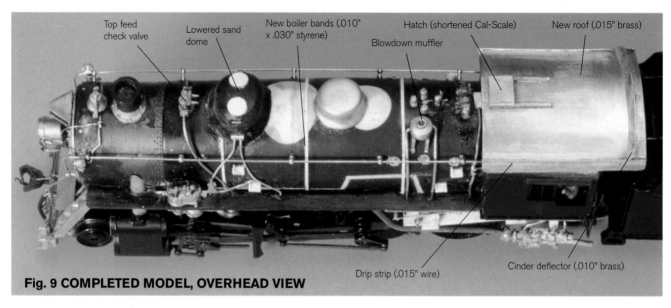

Top feed check valve

Lowered sand dome

New boiler bands (.010" x .030" styrene)

Hatch (shortened Cal-Scale)

Blowdown muffler

New roof (.015" brass)

Drip strip (.015" wire)

Cinder deflector (.010" brass)

Fig. 9 COMPLETED MODEL, OVERHEAD VIEW

Fig. 10 FRONT VIEW

Number board (Miniatures by Eric)

Marker lamps

Boiler stays (.028" wire)

Pilot step

Uncoupling lever

boiler stays made from .028" wire.

I made a new uncoupling lever from .015" wire and held it in place with the original Bachmann brackets. The air, train, and signal lines were cobbled up from fine single-core telephone wire with the insulation left in place, but you could substitute Cal-Scale parts. The coupler is held in place with a nut and washer screwed to the shaft of the 2-56 coupler mounting pin.

Firebox and ashpan

By the postwar era, the Central Vermont 2-8-0s had self-cleaning ashpans that wrapped around the firebox sides. These are quite noticeable in prototype photos (see fig. 7).

After cutting the firebox sides at a shallow angle to match the gentler rake of the prototype firebox, I built a new ashpan (see fig. 8). The sides are .125"-square styrene strip with the edges rounded. I cemented these in place along the lower edges of the firebox. Then I fabricated two rectangular doors from .010" styrene. Once these were attached to the sides, I filled the gaps with putty and sanded everything to shape once the putty had hardened.

Cab

The Bachmann cab is reasonably close to the prototype, but the arch of the roof is too high. After cutting off the rear overhang of the cab roof with my jeweler's saw, I drilled ⅛" holes around the perimeter of the

Fig. 11 FIREMAN'S SIDE, FRONT

Handrails (.019" nickel-silver wire)

Air compressor

New steam pipes (Plastruct)

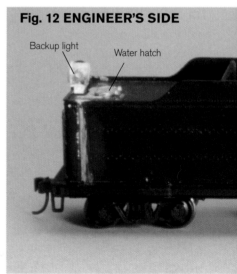

Fig. 12 ENGINEER'S SIDE

Backup light

Water hatch

roof and used Xuron micro-shears to cut out the roof pieces. All that was left were the cab sides and walls.

I filed the front and rear walls, leaving a much flatter curve in the middle of the roof. I did this by eye, following photographs, but you could make a template to ensure the curve radius is equal on both sides. I also removed the raised plate on the cab sides.

The new roof is .015" sheet brass. After cutting it to length, I bent it to shape, taking care to match the curvature of the front and rear cab walls. The new roof was carefully filed to achieve a good fit over the cab windows.

I soldered on .015" wire drip strips and shortened a Cal-Scale roof hatch before soldering it in place (see fig. 9). Next I cut the cinder deflector from .010" brass sheet and filed it to fit. With the deflector soldered in place, I glued the new roof in position with gap-filling CA. I used body putty to fill the joint between the roof and the cab sides.

Running boards

New running boards, made from .040" styrene, were the next job. I held a sheet of .040" styrene against the boiler and marked the boiler contour on the plastic before cutting the running boards to the proper width.

Start with the engineer's side since the running board only has to be trimmed to fit around the steam pipe. On the fireman's side, the running board has to be cut to fit around the compressor and, on some locomotives, the Worthington feedwater heater.

I added the piping to the compressor and glued it to the boiler with CA. I secured the running boards to the boiler with Plastic Weld and used some .040"-square styrene braces under the running board to hold it in place.

Smokebox front

The Cal-Scale smokebox front listed in the bill of materials (see page 27) isn't an exact match for the prototype, but it's the closest I could find. I drilled the smokebox front (see fig. 10) to take the headlight bulb wires, handrail stanchions, and mounting pins for the headlight bracket and number board.

To achieve a good fit between the smokebox front and smokebox, I placed the front face up on a large mill file and rubbed vigorously, reducing the thickness of the brass and producing a flat surface. I used epoxy to attach the front to the boiler.

Boiler details

To see the details I added to the boiler, refer to figs. 11, 12, and 13. While I used CA to attach new brass parts to the plastic model, I held plastic parts in place using liquid cement. I soldered brass wire to the brass details prior to attaching the

Fig. 13 FIREMAN'S SIDE, REAR

Blowdown muffler

Nathan injector starter valve

Elesco exhaust steam injector

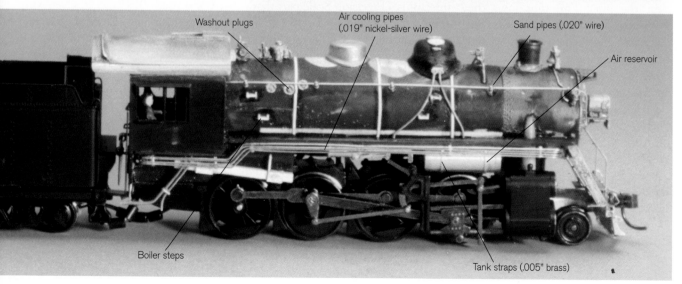

Washout plugs

Air cooling pipes (.019" nickel-silver wire)

Sand pipes (.020" wire)

Air reservoir

Boiler steps

Tank straps (.005" brass)

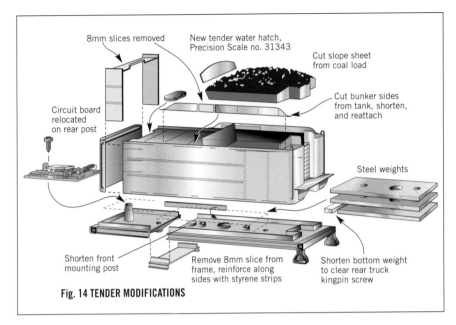

8mm slices removed

New tender water hatch, Precision Scale no. 31343

Cut slope sheet from coal load

Cut bunker sides from tank, shorten, and reattach

Circuit board relocated on rear post

Steel weights

Shorten front mounting post

Remove 8mm slice from frame, reinforce along sides with styrene strips

Shorten bottom weight to clear rear truck kingpin screw

Fig. 14 TENDER MODIFICATIONS

Fig. 15 TENDER. The shortened tender still has enough room for the Bachmann circuit board. No. 472 was equipped with a SoundTraxx steam sound decoder and a speaker and put to work on the layout.

subassembly to the engine model.

After adding the new boiler bands (.010" x .030" styrene) and bell, I turned my attention to the stack.

I cut the Bachmann stack 5mm down from the cap and removed the mold parting line before securing the shortened barrel into a Precision Scale brass base.

The cut-down sand dome is centered 40mm back from the boiler front, with the steam dome 24mm farther back.

I fitted the top feed check valve with pipes made from .025" brass wire. I marked where the end of the pipe met the fireman's side running board and drilled a hole from the underside of the running board to clear the pipe. This pipe joins the feedwater heater plumbing. On the engineer's side, the pipe is routed beneath the boiler jacket. I bent it down to meet the boiler and drilled an oblique hole to take it.

I drilled the holes for the washout plugs slightly undersized and carefully reamed them until the plugs sat flush with the boiler.

I placed the blowdown muffler on the fireman's side, but at least one N-5a, no. 471, had the muffler on the engineer's side.

I made my own boiler steps from Plastruct I beam, but I recommend using the Precision Scale part listed in the bill of materials (cut the lower mounting strap from the PSC part). I ended up flinging so many of the plastic steps from my tweezers, I'm still finding CV 2-8-0 boiler steps scattered around the workshop.

Piping

Most of the piping is Detail Associates wire of the appropriate diameter. The Nathan injector starter valve on the fireman's side (see fig. 13) just in front of the cab, was cobbled from bits of wire, but Cal-Scale has a casting (no. 293) which is pretty close.

The massive Elesco exhaust steam injector is a Precision Scale part that's a pretty fair stand-in for the appliance found on the CV locomotives.

The large feedpipe below the running board is thick copper wire. The injector is mounted to a bracket from .125"-square styrene secured to the cab floor with liquid cement.

Moving to the engineer's side of the engine (see fig. 12), the power reverse is a simple Alco type located under the running board beneath the steam dome. I attached a piece of .060" styrene to the underside of the running board to provide a firm mounting for the power reverse.

To duplicate the prototype's fairly large diameter air tank, I used one from Precision Scale (no. 31058). I cut the tube 18mm long and soldered the ends in place. Then I added the straps (.005" brass strip) and cemented the tank beneath the running board.

I made the air-cooling pipes from .019" nickel-silver wire, which was really too springy for the job. Brass wire is a better choice. I joined the four pipes into a unit with brackets of fine brass strip, then soldered the whole assembly to two short lengths of .028" wire which serve as mounting brackets. The wire was glued to the smokebox and cab with CA.

I also used .019" nickel-silver wire for the handrails. Once I got the handrail for one side bent to shape, I used it as a pattern for the other side. The stanchions are Japanese items made for the British market that I had in my scrap box, but Precision Scale no. 371 stanchions will also work.

Central Vermont steamers, like their Canadian National cousins, had handrails that went all the way down to the pilot beam with a cross brace between the two side handrails positioned just below the headlight. I cheated a little and cut the handrails

a fraction short so the pilot could be separated from the boiler without twisting the delicate handrails.

After soldering the cross brace in place, I reassembled the locomotive and tender for testing. I crossed my fingers, placed the engine on the track, and turned up the throttle. By some miracle, everything still worked. With the locomotive ready to go, I turned my attention to the tender.

Tender

An accurate CV tender would be a scratchbuilding job. As that goes beyond the scope of this project, I modified the Bachmann tender to get as close to the prototype as possible.

Figure 14 shows how I modified the tender. Start by removing the body from the frame and then remove the circuit board.

After removing the coal load. I cut the body along the vertical seams at the rear of each side, then cut across the deck to remove the rear wall. Next, I sliced an 8mm section from the sides and deck. After I cut away the molded hatch and patched the resulting hole in the deck with .040" styrene, I sanded both parts of the tender on a sanding block and glued the two sections together, reinforcing the joint with a piece of .015" styrene.

I reattached the rear of the tender to the rest of the body, again reinforcing the joints with .015" styrene. I filled the gap with putty and allowed it to dry. Then I added a backup light

(mounted on a small styrene bracket) and a water hatch to the train's tender.

To shorten the frame, I removed the rear truck and weights. I cut the frame immediately behind the front mounting post and trimmed the post so it protruded no higher than the weights.

I took the rear section of the frame, shortened it by 8mm, and filed it to get a good fit. After cementing the two halves together, I used .030" styrene to reinforce the joint.

Next I refitted the rear truck, making sure the insulated wheels were on the opposite side from those on the front truck. After shortening the bottom weight by 8mm to clear the rear truck kingpin screw and nut, I then firmly attached the weights to the floor with contact cement.

I simply replaced the Bachmann circuit board but, since then, a SoundTraxx steam sound decoder and speaker has been installed in the tender (see fig. 15).

A long trip to the paint shop

The completed model certainly has the air of a CV Consolidation. I shipped the engine to Waukesha, Wis., where the *Model Railroader* staff covered all the scars with a CV paint job (see Bill of Materials).

Finishing touches

(by Marty McGuirk, former associate editor, *Model Railroader*)

I was rather impressed with my

ability to convince Iain Rice to build a CV 2-8-0 for me, but I couldn't convince him to paint and decal the model as well.

I airbrushed the locomotive and tender with a mix of four parts Polly Scale Steam Power Black and one part Boxcar Red. This produces a warm black that looks good in person and in photos.

After the black dried, I used a brush to paint the smokebox. For this I used a custom "Light Graphite" color—a 1:1 mix of Polly Scale BAR Gray and Santa Fe Silver. I used a small paintbrush to apply this color. Wet the brush before dipping it in the paint and you'll find the paint flows much better.

Compared to the prototype photos, my smokebox looked too new, so I weathered it using powdered black pastel chalk.

The lettering is made from Microscale CV steam locomotive decals. Since I model the 1950s, I used the red tender monogram from that period. Central Vermont locomotives painted prior to 1943 had tender heralds with green backgrounds.

I added some final weathering, primarily heavily diluted (nine parts thinner to one part paint) Grimy Black and Earth, along with a load of Scenic Express coal (which hides the speaker and muffles the sound slightly), and no. 472 was ready for service. Now all I need is four or five more just like it!

FOUR Detailing the Bowser HO Pennsy I1 Decapod

Modeling two versions of this classic workhorse locomotive

Chaz Hammond

By Frank A. Costanzi
Photos by the author

In 1995 Bowser announced a new Pennsylvania RR I1 Decapod, replacing the firm's earlier version with a too skinny boiler. I was impressed enough to buy two, along with Bowser's superdetailing kits. After adding details by other manufacturers I ended up with two variations.

My main reference was photos in Alvin F. Staufer's book, *Pennsy Power.* Also, I found photographs and a drawing of the engineer's side in *Model Railroader Cyclopedia: Vol. 1, Steam Locomotives,* published by Kalmbach. I had to guess where some of the parts went, but the explanations of pumps, air systems, feedwater heater systems, and the like in the *Cyclopedia* helped make those guesses educated.

Besides the usual tools—small drills, files, a scribe—you will need a wheel puller and a quarterer from NorthWest Short Line. These are not very expensive, but are absolutely essential for producing a smooth running locomotive.

Follow Bowser's drawings, although a few discrepancies exist between

them and other drawings and photos, which I'll point out. The Pennsy may have been the "Standard Railroad of the World," but as the nearly 600 I1 engines repeatedly went in and out of the shops over some 40 years, many variations came to be known.

I drilled all the mounting holes before fastening any parts to the boiler, minimizing the opportunities for damage. Use a go-slow approach—drill a little, check the fit, and do it again. Use a scribe and center punch to mark and start the holes. And should you make a mistake (I made lots), just remember, Squadron putty and a little paint cover a multitude of sins.

Repowering

With the cover plate on, lengthen the gear slot in the frame to accommodate the NorthWest Short Line gearbox, keeping the axle holes on the frame and gearbox aligned. Remove the cover plate and file grooves in the frame to clear the screw heads on the gearbox.

I bent and drilled the brass mounting foot for the kit's Pittman motor to fit a Sagami (see fig. 1). Elongate the motor

Author Frank Costanzi detailed two versions of the Pennsylvania RR's class I1 2-10-0 Decapods starting with Bowser's HO kits. Number 4510, shown above, has a long tender and air pumps on both sides of the engine. Frank's other engine appears in fig. 2.

mounting hole (behind the last driver) to accommodate the new motor.

Using the NWSL gear puller and quarterer, replace the Bowser gear on the main axle with the one from the gearbox kit. Re-quartering the remaining drivers is a good idea, as Bowser's quartering jig may not match yours. To ensure proper quartering, I removed both wheels on each axle, as the axles are knurled and the knurling tends to force the previous alignment.

Mount the drivers in the frame, attach the side rods, and check for binding. If you find any, check the quartering. Do not enlarge the holes on the side rods, as that might make matters worse.

Mount the motor. Complete the flywheel/motor/gearbox assembly. Shim the worm so there is no play in

Don Wood

The I1s were distinctive for their large twin air tanks mounted on the pilot. Note the engine in this 1956 photo does not have an air pump on the engineer's side.

firebox should be spaced with the center plug midway between the cab and the front of the firebox, and the other two about five feet in front and behind.

Both Cal-Scale and Precision Scale make castings for other models of power reverses. You may wish to use a more modern model, particularly if your engine is post World War II.

The superdetail kit contains two starter valves and one injector. Early photographs of I1s show injectors and check valves located on the boiler backhead, a common Pennsy practice. Later the injectors often appeared under the cab sides. You can only be sure if you work from photos of a specific prototype. I also added water intake and overflow pipes under the cab sides, as well as air lines.

My scrap box (old N scale stuff really) provided the engineer's front side window, but just about any window sash of about that size and shape should suffice. For variety, I modeled the window partially open.

All the photos I have seen of Pennsy locos equipped with electric lights show what appears to be a valve and a small bit of piping from the steam dome to the top of the boiler, disappearing beneath the lagging. I believe this is a steam delivery line to the generator.

When mounting the sander valves, first file a bit of the sand dome flat to make a good seat for the valve casting, then proceed to drill. The Bowser drawing locates the forward sander pipes on both sides a bit too far back to clear the front drivers. Be sure to drill the hole for the rearward sander pipe in front of the location of the rear support for the power reverse.

The boiler: fireman's side

The Bowser illustration shows the stoker motor and the injector too far back. Align the injector so the delivery pipe runs up through the cab floor along the backhead. The stoker should be slightly behind the center of the cab window. Cut off the cast pipe at the bottom of the starter valve and use a no. 65 drill to seat the pipe from the injector.

the gearbox, and mount the gearbox as close to the motor as possible without binding. Lubricate. Rig some temporary wiring, and run the engine a while to ensure smooth operation.

Brakes and the engineer's side

First we'll build engine no. 4638 (short tender, air pumps on the fireman's side only), then we'll turn to engine 4510 and examine the differences.

Drill no. 70 mounting holes in the bottom plate, equally spaced between

the drivers, and fasten the brakes for the forward four pairs of drivers with cyanoacrylate adhesive (CA) (see fig. 2). Drill for and add the rear brakes.

Except for the handrail on the smokebox front and the one running the length of the boiler, which appear to be about right, I used .015" steel wire rather than the .020" brass wire in the kit. The smaller wire looks in better proportion and steel is less susceptible to bending with handling.

Contrary to the Bowser drawings, the washout plugs on each side of the

Fig. 1 MECHANISM. Frank replaced the kit motor and gearbox with a Sagami motor and NorthWest Short Line gearbox.

Not all I1s were equipped with blowdown mufflers, so mounting the one provided with the superdetail kit is optional. I decided to add it. The holes (no. 65) in the running board provide a good spot to mate pipes and hide the joints.

The small pipe (.020") from the steam turret down alongside the starter valve should also be led forward to the vicinity of the steam chest. The mechanism mounting block (part no. 70303) becomes part of the steam chest when the model is assembled; much of the piping running forward can be conveniently mounted to it.

I provided the fireman with extra ventilation via an open cab-front door. Drilling a few holes followed by some patient filing provided the opening. I thinned and trimmed a Precision Scale door to fit and cemented it in place with CA after I'd painted the model.

Feedwater heater

The feedwater heater supplied by Bowser appears to be a model BL4, but the photos I have seen picture an earlier—and slightly narrower—model BL or BL2. Unfortunately, I noticed this difference a bit late in the game. I was ready to start painting and decided that changing out feedwater heaters at this point was just not worth the effort.

On I1s, the Pennsy generally ran the steam pipe to the feedwater heater pump from inside the cab. To add mine, I drilled a no. 58 hole in the cab front to the inside and slightly above the fireman's door, just enough above the line of rivets to clear the handrail.

Add an exhaust steam line from behind the feedwater heater pump to the top of the heater check valve, as shown in fig. 3. Also shown is exhaust steam piping from the steam chest to the bottom of the pump check valve. I used a piece of steam pipe from a casting I found in a junk box at a hobby shop, but both Cal-Scale and Precision Scale make Worthington BL feedwater heaters that have this bit of pipe included. I drilled a no. 75 hole in both the bottom of the check valve

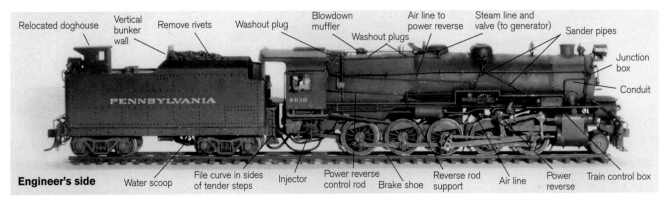

Engineer's side

Relocated doghouse — Vertical bunker wall — Remove rivets — Washout plug — Blowdown muffler — Washout plugs — Air line to power reverse — Steam line and valve (to generator) — Sander pipes — Junction box — Conduit

Water scoop — File curve in sides of tender steps — Injector — Power reverse control rod — Brake shoe — Reverse rod support — Air line — Power reverse — Train control box

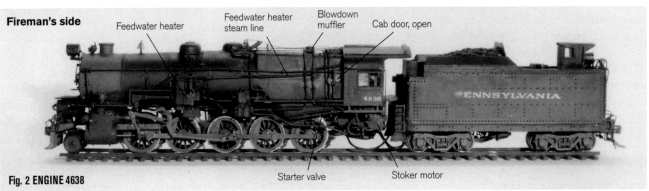

Fireman's side

Feedwater heater — Feedwater heater steam line — Blowdown muffler — Cab door, open

Starter valve — Stoker motor

Fig. 2 ENGINE 4638

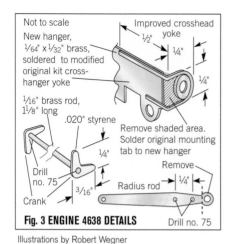

Not to scale

New hanger,
$1/64$" x $1/32$" brass,
soldered to modified
original kit cross-hanger yoke

Improved crosshead
yoke

$1/2$"

$1/4$"

$1/4$"

$1/16$" brass rod,
$1^{1}/8$" long

.020" styrene

$1/4$"

Remove shaded area.
Solder original mounting
tab to new hanger

Drill
no. 75

Remove

$1/4$"

Crank

$3/16$"

Radius rod

Drill no. 75

Fig. 3 ENGINE 4638 DETAILS

Illustrations by Robert Wegner

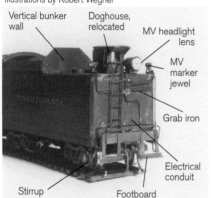

Vertical bunker
wall

Doghouse,
relocated

MV headlight
lens

MV
marker
jewel

Grab iron

Electrical
conduit

Stirrup

Footboard

Generator

Pipe, .032" wire

Reverse lever

Feedwater heater steam line

$1/16$" hole for
headlight wires

Lifting link

Sander air line

Whistle

Lubrication lines

Pipe and valve

Steam delivery pipe

Necking
filed in

Added exhaust steam pipe

Radius rod

Crosshead
hanger

Feedwater heater

Air delivery

Eccentric crank

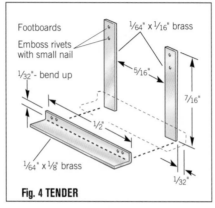

Footboards

Emboss rivets
with small nail

$1/64$" x $1/16$" brass

$1/32$"- bend up

$5/16$"

$7/16$"

$1/2$"

$1/64$" x $1/8$" brass

$1/32$"

Fig. 4 TENDER

and the top of the pipe and used a short piece of .020" wire as a dowel to align the parts as I secured them with a bit of CA.

More details

Drill holes for the stanchions and the cylinder lubrication lines. Photographs of the fireman's side show what appears to be a stop cock and pipe just forward of the cylinder steam delivery pipe. I simulated it by fastening a short piece of .020" brass wire to the side of a stop cock casting, but waited until I had positioned the steam delivery pipe before drilling a hole for this part.

The Bowser illustrations are not clear as to where the fill lids go on the sand dome, but this is clearly indicated in the *MR Cyclopedia* drawing. They ended up $3/16$" either side of the boiler center line.

A $1/16$" hole angled through the front edge of the smokebox front accommodates the necessary wiring for the headlight.

Adding parts and piping

Start securing parts with a very small amount of gap-filling CA. You may wish to detail the smokebox front last to minimize danger to the delicate steps. Also, mount the generator to the smokebox front after the handrail over the boiler top is mounted.

Examine the illustrations and diagrams carefully to determine which parts to mount first, as some parts end up under others.

Attaching the air lines under the running boards is a bit tricky owing to all the bends. I found it easiest to first attach the middle hanger to the underside of the running board, then thread the .020" wires though it. Slip the rear and forward hangers onto the wires, make the appropriate bends, then secure the hangers to the boiler.

Because the sander pipes run on either side of the handrail stanchion below the sand dome, I temporarily inserted the stanchion into its hole to ensure clearance. Also I used .025" brass wire for the sander pipes, rather than the .032" wire provided.

To model the feedwater intake pipe, wedge a length of $1/16$" brass wire between the feedwater heater and running board and cement it to the inside of the air pump. For the pipe running from near the steam chest and alongside the feedwater line to under the cab, I used .032" wire.

Fit a length of .032" wire for the water delivery pipe from the bottom inside of the feedwater heater to mate with the hot water pipe where it penetrates the running board.

On the engineer's side run conduit from the junction box to the train control box under the running board. If your I1 is an early model sans train control (early '20s), then you will not need this conduit. However, you will need to remove the portion of upper running board overlapping the lower. Further, you will need to mount a Cal-Scale damper control just above the running board at the joint between the smokebox and boiler.

On some engines the handrails ran straight through the cab front; on others they ended at the last stanchion. On some engines, on the engineer's side, the handrail curved up from the last stanchion to a junction box above the cab front window. (Handrails doubled as conduit for electrical wires.)

Cylinders

Remove the mold taper from the cylinder castings with a flat file. On most I1s the front and rear of the valve chambers were necked. A bit of filing will reproduce this feature.

Many photos show a capped pipe

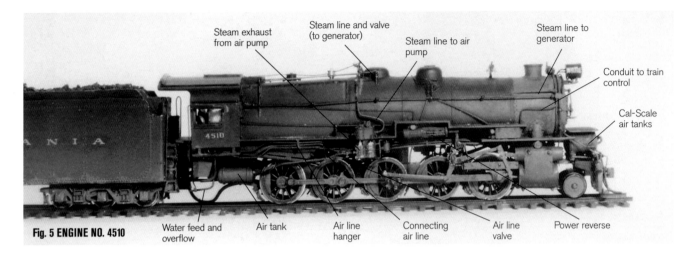

Fig. 5 ENGINE NO. 4510

Labels: Steam exhaust from air pump · Steam line and valve (to generator) · Steam line to air pump · Steam line to generator · Conduit to train control · Cal-Scale air tanks · Water feed and overflow · Air tank · Air line hanger · Connecting air line · Air line valve · Power reverse

protruding from the lower portion of the cylinder head. Usually this appears on the front, sometimes on the rear, and sometimes not at all—a hole in the cylinder head cover being all that remains. I used scraps of plastic sprue, filed in the shape of the plug and bolts, to simulate these objects on one locomotive, but drilled holes in the cylinder face for the other—I just got weary.

Bowser has located the holes and bushings for the piston rods outside of the cylinder center lines, presumably to ensure clearance between the crosshead and side rods. To locate my piston rods on center, I first removed and discarded the bushings. Then I filled the cavity with Squadron putty, leaving a short piece of .045" wire pressed to the inside. Once the putty cured, I removed the wire and sanded the area smooth. I have not had any clearance problems.

The superdetail kit instructions call for a no. 65 drill to join the steam delivery pipe to the cylinder casting, but I found that a no. 61 afforded a bit of slop that allowed a better seating.

Valve gear

To make a better-looking crosshead yoke, I cut, filed, and added some brass flat stock until something more closely resembling the prototype emerged (see fig. 3). I also modified the radius rods both for appearance and to accommodate the reverse levers. I made the levers and cranks from .020" styrene and .020" wire stuck onto a length of $\frac{1}{16}$" brass rod and cemented to the hanger.

Bowser steps 1 and 2 for assembling the valve gear are incorrect. The combination lever (no. 8820) must be mounted outside the radius rod (no. 9840) and the valve rod (no. 8810), as correctly shown in steps 3, 4, and 5.

With some drilling and filing, the eccentric crank that Bowser makes for its Challenger and Big Boy locomotives can be made fairly credible. The hex screw (no. 804) serves as

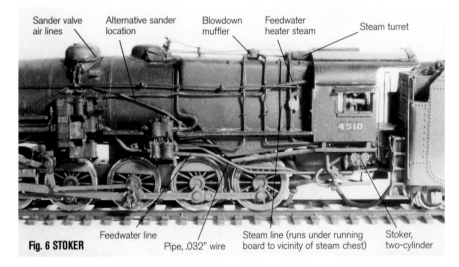

Fig. 6 STOKER

Labels: Sander valve air lines · Alternative sander location · Blowdown muffler · Feedwater heater steam · Steam turret · Feedwater line · Pipe, .032" wire · Steam line (runs under running board to vicinity of steam chest) · Stoker, two-cylinder

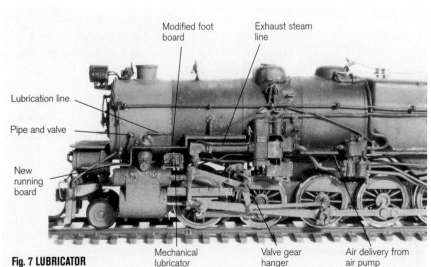

Fig. 7 LUBRICATOR

Labels: Modified foot board · Exhaust steam line · Lubrication line · Pipe and valve · New running board · Mechanical lubricator · Valve gear hanger · Air delivery from air pump

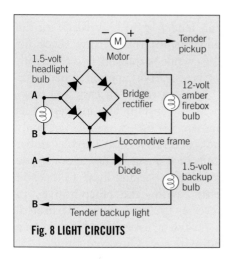

Fig. 8 LIGHT CIRCUITS

the main crank pin and you'll need to file the head down, as the pins that come with the cranks are too large to accommodate the main crank spacer (no. 874). I wrapped the screw in paper so as not to damage the threads, secured it in a drill chuck, and turned it with a file.

Final assembly (almost)

Follow Bowser's instructions and assemble the locomotive, omitting the cylinder steam delivery pipes, bell, whistle, number plate, backhead, cab rear, pop valves, headlight, pilot, and engineer and fireman. You just want to be sure everything still works smoothly before you have applied that super paint job and weathered your engine to look as if it has spent the last two years shoving coal to Sodus Point.

Before you disassemble for painting, attach the steam delivery pipes and the pipe in front of the steam delivery pipe on the fireman's side.

Replace the Bowser air tanks for the pilot with a Cary casting. Now attach the pilot to the frame with the motor-mounting bolt and a 2-56 nut, running the bolt through a Kadee no. 5 coupler draft gear box minus its ears. File the footboard supports thinner.

Tender

The tender provided is more like the 90-F-75 tender used behind an L1 Mikado. The major visual discrepancies include the absence of a

well for the brakeman's doghouse, the deck height of 75" (82" would be correct), the water hatch being located between the doghouse and the rear of the coal bunker, and the absence of rear footboards.

I moved the doghouse to a correct location, but didn't attempt to make a well for it. See fig. 4. I added the electrical junction box, fabricated pilot foot boards, made a few cosmetic changes (coming up), and declared victory.

Form the curves in the sides of the steps with a small round file. Next, bend the rear wall of the coal bunker vertical and fill the joint where it meets the top of the tender with

putty. With a small flat file, remove the rivets on the sloped portions of the tender sides. Remove the rear steps and add stirrups made from ¹⁄₆₄" x ¹⁄₁₆" brass stock.

I made a pair of footboards from brass stock, soldering the pieces together, but using CA to secure them to the rear beam after all the other tender detailing was complete.

Fill the doghouse mounting hole and the water hatch hole on the fireman's side with putty. The other predrilled hole can be used for wiring the backup light. Drill a no. 42 hole on center ⁹⁄₁₆" from the rear of the tender and remount the doghouse.

Cut the studs off the water hatch and glue them to the tender with CA.

Shim the light with .020" styrene so its face just hangs over the lip. Position the electrical conduits for the marker lamps and backup light. Add the grab iron to the right of the ladder.

Engine no. 4510

My second engine, shown in the color photo leading this article (see page 32), features a longhaul tender and a second air pump that was added to many of these engines as the air brake system was modernized. This pump went on the engineer's side and the air tank formerly occupying its place was moved back just ahead of the cab (see fig. 5).

You'll need to run a steam pipe over the top of the boiler to connect the two air pumps. You'll also need to run an exhaust steam line from the second air pump to the steam chest as well as an air line running from this pump to the middle air line under the running board. (This line connects to the air tank on the single-pump models.) The valve to isolate the pump is from the Cal-Scale set noted in the materials.

The relocated air tank will need some air lines, so before mounting it, drill holes in the ends to accommodate them, .020" rear and .032" front. Cement a scrap of styrene to the tank to mount the brakes for the rear driver.

I didn't mount an injector below the cab on the engineer's side, so I needed to add water intake and overflow pipes, as would be the case under any cab side where the injector is in the cab.

Photographs suggest two-cylinder stokers were used with the longhaul tenders. To so equip your engine, you will need to cut away part of the frame, boiler, and stoker casting itself to make it fit (see fig. 6). The boiler alteration is simple enough, but I suggest you wait until after all the holes have been drilled and parts fitted (though not mounted), as the wing to be removed affords some stability when working on the boiler.

As shown in fig. 7, this engine is also equipped with a mechanical lubricator, mounted on the steam chest, fireman's side, which required removing and modifying the entire lower front section of the running board. Save the removed section to provide the correct length of steam delivery pipe on this side.

Painting and final touches

Follow Bowser's directions to clean and pickle the parts. I used Polly Scale Brunswick Green for the boiler and tender body, Oily Black for the underframes, and Grimy Black for the cylinders, applying two coats with a two-day drying period in between.

You can make an easy and inexpensive constant lighting system as shown in fig. 8. While certainly not necessary, the 12-volt amber bulb provides a firebox glow. If you want the backup light to operate only with the locomotive in reverse, use a diode as illustrated.

Following assembly, I brushed on a bit of Testor's Glosscote, thinned 1:1 and applied in vertical strokes with a fairly broad brush to simulate streaking that occurs over time from rain.

After applying the kit decals, I weathered my locomotives with a bit of Rust-all and Weather-all. Final weathering was a light overall airbrushing with a mixture of Polly Scale Grimy Black and Mud. I mixed these two colors, adding a bit of one, then some of the other, until I achieved a color I liked—somewhat olive drab, but very pale. I applied the mixture very lightly over each locomotive, then blended it in toward the bottom so that the locomotive was dulled everywhere but only really dirty near the rails. It was time for these workhorses to start earning their keep.

KITBASHING
And Scratchbuilding

Most model railroaders are content to operate a steam engine as it comes from the box, perhaps adding a few details unique to the prototype being modeled. However, there are a number of modelers who cannot create what they want from anything that exists on the market. These modelers eventually achieve their goal in one of two ways. For some modelers, a desirable approach is to chop up and combine the parts from a number of different kits while adding other available details. This is called kitbashing. For others, there is simply no base locomotive that will work as a starting point. When this is the case, the modeler may scale down the prototype's plans and use brass structural shapes and sheets, along with commercial motors and detail parts, to make the locomotive of his dreams. This is called scratchbuilding.

Kitbashing and scratchbuilding were fairly common prior to the 1960s. Today, however, one might wonder why a modeler would want to spend the time, considering the variety of beautifully detailed plastic and brass steam locomotives on the market. The answers are pride and creativity. Despite the long hours and hard work, kitbashing and scratchbuilding are fun to some modelers, and there is a great deal of pride in creating an end product that is truly unique. Having scratchbuilt or kitbashed more than a dozen locomotives because there were no models of New Haven steam engines at the time, I can attest to both points.

In this chapter you'll find one extensive article on scratchbuilding a 4-6-0 in brass. While you may not be ready to tackle this level of construction today, at some point you may want to try your hand at it—the rewards are great. *John Pryke*

FIVE Building an HO 4-6-0 in brass

By Stephen Anderson
Photos by the author

From October 1997 through May 1998, Stephen Anderson wrote an eight-part article on scratchbuilding an HO 4-6-0 in brass for *Model Railroader* Magazine. The following pages contain excerpts from this series, including the key assembly drawings, photos, and scratchbuilding techniques. To obtain the complete, original series of articles, readers should request the October 1997 through May 1998 back issues of *Model Railroader* directly from Kalmbach Publishing.

Before starting construction, it is essential to have the proper tools for scratchbuilding in brass. On the next page, Stephen describes these tools and their use.

A good set of drawings and photographs of the prototype is essential when scratchbuilding. These may be found in current and past issues of magazines such as *Model Railroader*, books on the railroad on which the locomotive ran, railroad historical societies, and railroad photo dealers.

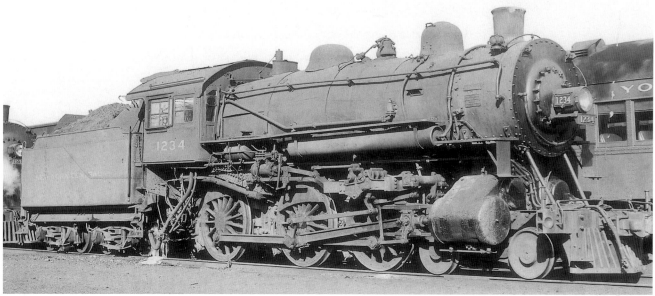

The NYC 1234 at Yorktown Heights, N.Y. in December 1950.

John P. Ahrens

When working with brass, you'll be measuring, marking, cutting, drilling, filing, and soldering. These require just a very small collection of tools. Most of the tools needed to construct a brass engine are shown in the photos.

• **The most useful tool** that I have found is a dial caliper because it shows, on an easy-to-read dial, the exact size to .001". A caliper of adequate quality costs about $30. Don't buy a plastic one, as you'll be using it as a scribe as well as a measuring device.

• **For laying out parts** you'll also need a center punch, a small machinist's square, and a scribe. Don't use your scribe as a center punch—you want the tip to stay sharp.

• **Good cutting tools** make all your work easier and better. A razor saw works fine for cutting brass, though it's rather slow. Not pictured is a jeweler's saw, which is shaped like a small coping saw and allows you to cut curves and complex shapes.

• **You'll use files** more than any other tool, so they should be the best quality you can find. For heavy cutting, you should have an 8" and a 6" mill file. Try to get these from a store that sells to industrial customers. They will cost a little more, but better files make the work go faster and easier.

• **A set of jeweler's** files is necessary for finishing small parts, the smaller the file the better. A set from Radio Shack is a good start, but try to get one high-quality square jeweler's file. High-quality files have smaller teeth and remain sharper longer.

A set of very small jeweler's files is also handy. None of these files is very expensive, but they are cutting tools and should be replaced when they become dull.

• **You'll need a set** of small numbered drills and a pin vise. Start with the tap and clearance drills of all the screw sizes used as shown in the chart at right. I use 00-90, 0-80, and 2-56. One tap for each of the screw sizes is also needed. Using a pin vise to drill holes gets old after a short time. I suggest getting a small precision power drill such as a Dremel Moto-Tool or hand unit.

• **A 40-watt iron** is adequate for almost all

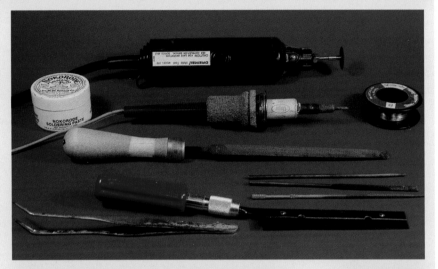

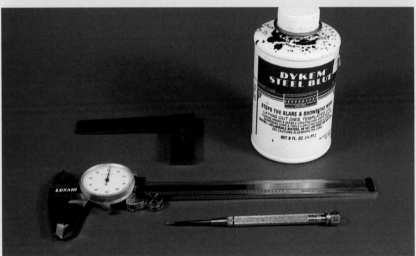

soldering. I use paste flux to clean the metal first. I recommend .025"- or .032"-diameter rosin-core solder. It may be helpful to have a 250-watt soldering gun, but I seldom use the one I have.

If your budget allows, you may want to add some tools to make your work faster and easier.

• **A drill press** is almost a necessity. A drill press stand for your motor tool will do. Next, I recommend a speed control for your motor tool. I made mine from a foot-operated sewing machine speed control which leaves both hands free.

• **The tool that saves** the most time and aggravation is a powered bench-type scroll saw. I use one to cut brass sheet

and rod. Though not necessary, it can reduce an hour-long cutting job down to about a minute.

• **A small lathe** such as a Preac, Sherline, or Unimat is a good investment, especially if you want to build cylinders, domes, and other complex parts.

Drill and tap sizes		
Screw size	Tap drill	Clearance drill
00-90	61	55
0-80	55	52
2-56	50	43

Translating prototype dimensions to the size of a model's parts is a key step in scratchbuilding a locomotive. On the next page, Stephen describes how to do this using Microsoft Excel or by using a Modelcalc calculator.

Knowing how to cut and square sheet brass is important in fabricating parts, see below.

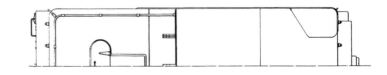

Drawn for *Model Railroader* Magazine
by J. Harold Geissel

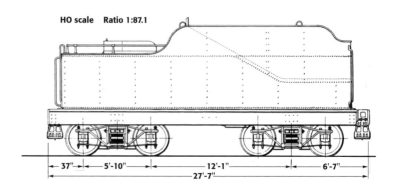

HO scale   Ratio 1:87.1

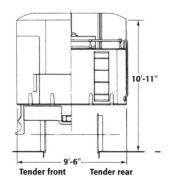

10'-11"

9'-6"

Tender front   **Tender rear**

37"   5'-10"   12'-1"   6'-7"
27'-7"

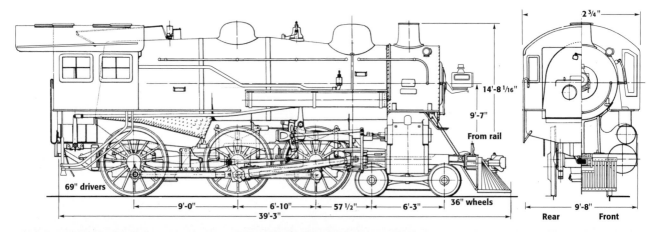

2 3/4"

14'-8 1/16"

9'-7"
From rail

69" drivers

9'-0"   6'-10"   57 1/2"   6'-3"   36" wheels
39'-3"

9'-8"
Rear   **Front**

Basic techniques: squaring and cutting sheet metal

• **To square brass sheet,** file one edge perfectly straight with a 6" or 8" file. Don't assume the edge from the factory is straight!

Now coat the piece with machinist's dye—this allows you to scribe lines as easily as using a pencil. Using a small machinist's square, scribe a line very close to one end and perpendicular to the edge you filed straight. Now file the end to this line using your 8" file. You now have two edges that are straight and perpendicular to one another. From these, you can make accurate measurements to locate holes or lay out the shape of the part you're making.

• **Cutting heavy stock, .032"** and above, is best done with a saw (razor, jeweler's, or powered fret saw). A disk cutter in a motor tool is very useful for cutting bar stock to length and can also be used to cut sheet metal, but always wear eye and face protection: Disks break easily and flying pieces can cause serious injury.

For thinner stock, rough-cut the piece with metal shears (or even scissors) by gradually cutting small slivers off each edge. This method ensures that the sheet metal doesn't curl or distort from the shearing action.

Finish shaping the part with files. Use an 8" file for straight edges and jeweler's files for curves and final finish.

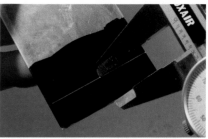

Use a dial caliper as a scribe. A dial caliper is a useful tool for laying out straight lines. Place the lower jaw against the edge of the brass, and draw the caliper along the edge of the sheet. Keep the caliper perpendicular to the edge for an accurate measurement.

Prototype drawings are dimensioned in actual feet and inches. These must be converted to the actual dimensions of the model, or you must measure everything with a scale rule. While the latter is possible, it's much easier to use regular tools marked in real inches.

To do this easily, I made a conversion chart with Microsoft Excel, a spreadsheet program. I loaded the cells with the following formulas to calculate actual dimensions for the scale equivalents from 1 inch to 13 actual feet. Part of this chart is printed below.

Column	Formula
1	Inches (1 to 156)
2	(column 1) mod 12 (feet)
3	(column 1) div/12 (inches)
4	(column 1)/87
	(model actual inches)

You can also do these conversions on a standard calculator. Convert the prototype dimension to inches and divide by 87.1.

This process is made even simpler if you purchase a ModelCalc from Calculated Industries. This calculator has built-in scale tables, so you can enter the prototype dimension in feet and inches (or meters and centimeters) and then press just one button to get the conversion.

Conversion table from Excel spreadsheet

Inches	Feet	Inches	Actual Inches	Inches	Feet	Inches	Actual	Inches	Feet	Inches	Actual
1	0	1	0.011	28	2	4	0.322	57	4	9	0.655
2	0	2	0.023	29	2	5	0.333	58	4	10	0.667
3	0	3	0.034	30	2	6	0.345	59	4	11	0.678
4	0	4	0.046	31	2	7	0.356	60	5	0	0.690
5	0	5	0.057	32	2	8	0.368	61	5	1	0.701
6	0	6	0.069	33	2	9	0.379	62	5	2	0.713
7	0	7	0.080	34	2	10	0.391	63	5	3	0.724
8	0	8	0.092	35	2	11	0.402	64	5	4	0.736
9	0	9	0.103	36	3	0	0.414	65	5	5	0.747
10	0	10	0.115	37	3	1	0.425	66	5	6	0.759
11	0	11	0.126	38	3	2	0.437	67	5	7	0.770
12	1	0	0.138	39	3	3	0.448	68	5	8	0.782
13	1	1	0.149	40	3	4	0.460	69	5	9	0.793
14	1	2	0.161	41	3	5	0.471	70	5	10	0.805
15	1	3	0.172	42	3	6	0.483	71	5	11	0.816
16	1	4	0.184	43	3	7	0.494	72	6	0	0.828
17	1	5	0.195	44	3	8	0.506	73	6	1	0.839
18	1	6	0.207	45	3	9	0.517	74	6	2	0.851
19	1	7	0.218	46	3	10	0.529	75	6	3	0.862
20	1	8	0.230	47	3	11	0.540	76	6	4	0.874
21	1	9	0.241	48	4	0	0.552	77	6	5	0.885
22	1	10	0.253	49	4	1	0.563	78	6	6	0.897
23	1	11	0.264	50	4	2	0.575	79	6	7	0.908
24	2	0	0.276	51	4	3	0.586	80	6	8	0.920
25	2	1	0.287	52	4	4	0.598	81	6	9	0.931
26	2	2	0.299	53	4	5	0.609	82	6	10	0.943
27	2	3	0.310	54	4	6	0.621	83	6	11	0.954
				55	4	7	0.632	84	7	0	0.966
				56	4	8	0.644	85	7	1	0.977

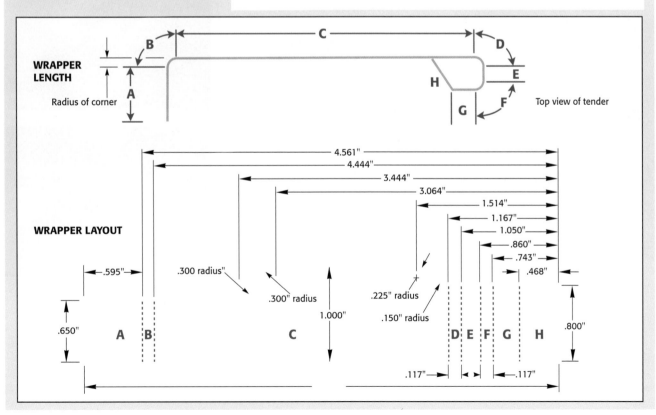

WRAPPER LENGTH

Radius of corner

Top view of tender

WRAPPER LAYOUT

.595"

.300 radius"

.300" radius

.225" radius

.150" radius

4.561"

4.444"

3.444"

3.064"

1.514"

1.167"

1.050"

.860"

.743"

.468"

.650"

A B

1.000"

C

D E F G H

.800"

.117"

.117"

Basic techniques: drilling and tapping

• **Drilling an accurately** located and sized hole usually requires progressive drilling. That means starting with a small pilot drill and gradually enlarging the hole to its final size.

For example, to drill a no. 55 hole, start by carefully drilling a no. 66 pilot hole. Use plenty of light oil on the bit as you drill. Remove the drill often to clear the chips that build up on the cutting edge. Then enlarge the hole first with a no. 60 bit and finish with the no. 55. This technique takes a few minutes longer but it is well worth the effort.

• **Tapping a hole** (cutting the threads for the screws) in brass is not difficult if you are careful. The taps we use are very tiny, but if used with care they will tap many holes. There are two drill sizes associated with tapping, called the tap drill and clearance drill.

The tap drill makes a hole slightly smaller than the outside diameter of the threads. It is this hole that you actually tap.

When tapping a hole, use plenty of light oil and remove the tap often and clean all chips from the tap by moving it across your finger. Use light pressure on the tap. You should never have to force a tap; good taps cut easily. Also, periodically reversing the tap a quarter turn frees chips from the cutting edges and makes tapping easier.

I would remove and clean the tap for a small hole at least three times while tapping it. If you think this is tedious, remember there's nothing more frustrating than breaking a tap in a hole and having to remake the entire part because you can't remove it.

The chart shows the tap and clearance drills for all the screws we'll be using to build this engine.

Basic techniques: soldering

There are several techniques for soldering, but all require that the parts be clean (free of paint, grime, and oils) and that you apply flux (rosin paste flux is my preference). For most work I find a 40-watt iron sufficient.

I solder most of my parts together by first tinning one piece, as that makes for a neat, quick joint. To tin a part, apply flux where you want solder (that is where the two parts will be joined), then heat and flow solder over the area. The goal is a thin, even coat of solder.

To attach parts, flux the untinned piece, bring the parts together, and apply heat to the joint. Adding a little extra solder between the tip of the iron and the joint helps transfer heat and make a solid joint. I use .025"-diameter rosin-core solder for small work and .032"-diameter for larger pieces.

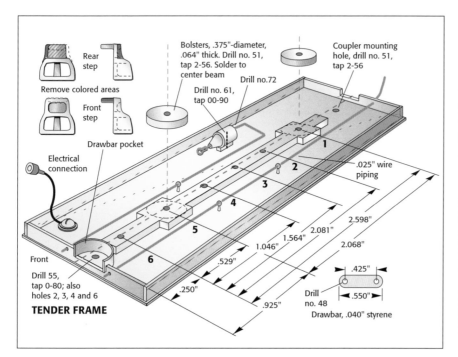

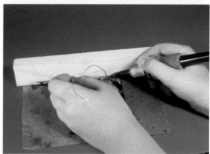

Top and above: This soldering jig is simply a 1" x 2" glued to a piece of Masonite. It allows you to hold parts together with one hand, so the other hand is free to use the iron.

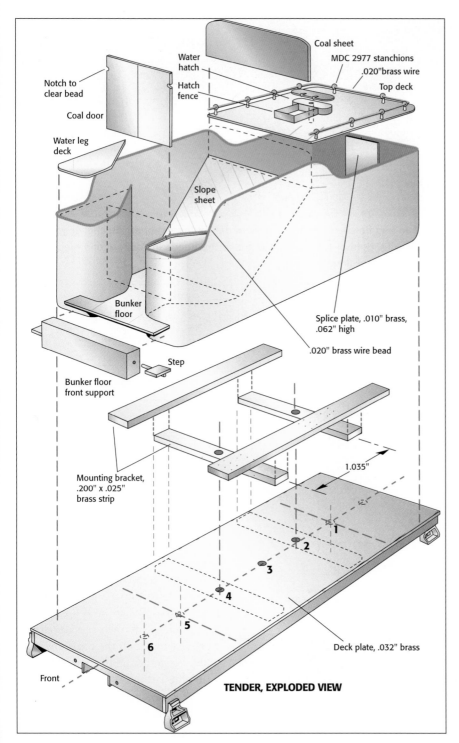

Notch to
clear bead

Coal door

Water leg
deck

Water
hatch

Hatch
fence

Coal sheet

MDC 2977 stanchions

.020" brass wire

Top deck

Slope
sheet

Bunker
floor

Bunker floor
front support

Step

Mounting bracket,
.200" x .025"
brass strip

Splice plate, .010" brass,
.062" high

.020" brass wire bead

1.035"

1

2

3

4

5

6

Deck plate, .032" brass

Front

TENDER, EXPLODED VIEW

Soldering is essential when assembling the brass parts of a scratchbuilt engine. Stephen shares his tips on how to solder a brass model at the upper right of page 44

As subassemblies take shape, many will be held together by machine screws. Stephen describes how he drills and taps screw holes at the upper left of page 44.

When scratchbuilding a locomotive, the tender is a good place to start, as it is the easiest part of the engine to design and assemble.

Exploded views are a very good way to help the builder envision how parts and subassemblies fit together to form a completed model. (See an exploded view of the tender in the diagram at left.)

Embossing rivets is critical for locomotive cabs, smoke boxes, and tenders. Below, Stephen shows how to use a scriber to create guidelines for the tender rivets, and a scale rule to space them. In thin brass (.005") the rivets can be embossed by hand with the point of a scriber. For thicker brass, using a small hammer to tap the scriber will work.

If you have a good drawing of a rivet pattern for a given part, tape it to the brass as a guide for embossing rivets.

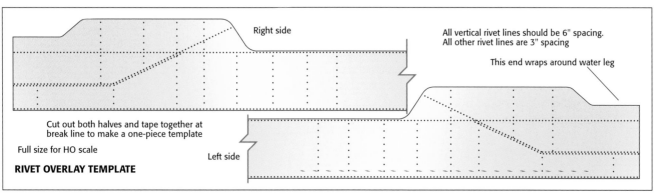

Right side

All vertical rivet lines should be 6" spacing.
All other rivet lines are 3" spacing

This end wraps around water leg

Cut out both halves and tape together at
break line to make a one-piece template

Full size for HO scale

Left side

RIVET OVERLAY TEMPLATE

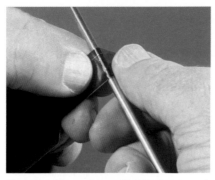

Bending the wrapper. Hold a brass rod between the corner bend lines of your wrapper and carefully bend around it. Keep the rod perpendicular to the sides, so the corners are square.

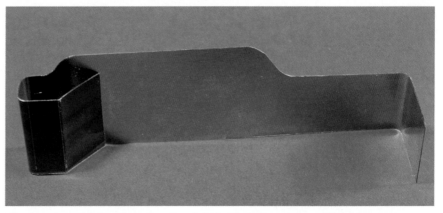

Stephen has finished bending the right half of the wrapper. Whichever you started with, right or left, be sure to make the bends in your second piece the opposite of your first.

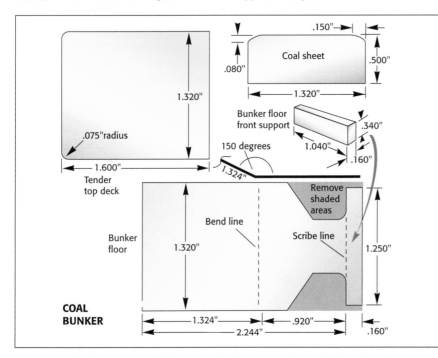

Tender top deck

1.320"
.075"radius
1.600"

Coal sheet
.150"
.080"
.500"
1.320"

Bunker floor front support
1.040"
.340"
.160"

150 degrees
1.324"

COAL BUNKER

Bunker floor
1.320"
Bend line
Remove shaded areas
Scribe line
1.250"

1.324"
.920"
.160"
2.244"

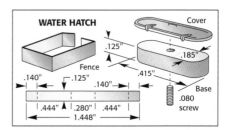

WATER HATCH
Cover
.125"
.185"
Fence
.415"
.140"
.125"
.140"
Base
.080 screw
.444"
.280"
.444"
1.448"

A variety of techniques can be used to shape brass parts. For example, Stephen uses a rod to bend a rounded corner.

With the tender's wrapper and floor complete, the coal bunker is the next part to be fabricated.

The final details (water hatch, ladders, handrails, etc.) are fabricated and installed last.

Holding onto parts being soldered together has always been a challenge to modelers. Stephen has developed a process in which the parts are "tack glued" together and then soldered. The glue is then removed with acetone. See his description of this technique to the left.

Basic techniques: glue, then solder

I developed this technique to keep parts that are difficult to hold or clamp in position perfectly aligned while soldering, for example the rear deck inside the wrapper.

Rather than trying to clamp it in place while making a neat solder joint, I first glue it in place with Duco cement from the top side. When the glue has dried (preferably overnight), I turn the assembly over, flux the joint, heat both the side and the deck and apply solder to the joint until it flows and forms a fillet. When the soldering is complete, I remove the cement from the top side with acetone.

This method takes longer than simply clamping so you don't want to use it for everything, but it's a life-saver for awkward pieces.

Stephen sharpened the ends of clothespins to make simple clamps to hold the bead. They also came in handy on other assemblies.

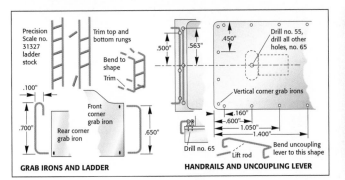

GRAB IRONS AND LADDER

Precision Scale no. 31327 ladder stock

Trim top and bottom rungs

Bend to shape

Trim

.100"

.700"

Rear corner grab iron

Front corner grab iron

.650"

Drill no. 55, drill all other holes, no. 65

.500"

.563"

.450"

Vertical corner grab irons

Drill no. 65

Lift rod

.160"

.600"

1.050"

1.400"

Bend uncoupling lever to this shape

HANDRAILS AND UNCOUPLING LEVER

At right is the completed tender. Stephen added just enough underbody detail to make its silhouette realistic when viewed from eye level.

The locomotive's drive train consists of a can motor driving a horizontal worm gear through a universal coupling as shown in the drawing below. All of these components are available from NorthWest Shortline.

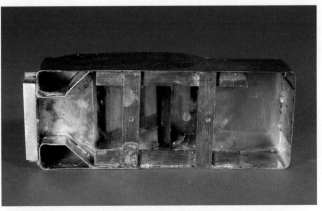

After the superstructure is located relative to the frame, glue the H shaped bracket in place, then remove the superstructure and bracket from the frame and solder together.

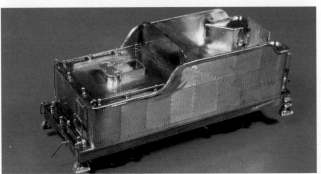

The two photos above show the completed tender.

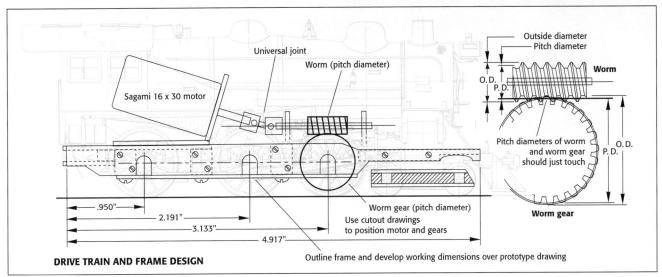

DRIVE TRAIN AND FRAME DESIGN

Sagami 16 x 30 motor

Universal joint

Worm (pitch diameter)

.950"

2.191"

3.133"

4.917"

Worm gear (pitch diameter)

Use cutout drawings to position motor and gears

Outline frame and develop working dimensions over prototype drawing

Outside diameter

Pitch diameter

Worm

O.D.

P.D.

Pitch diameters of worm and worm gear should just touch

O.D.

P.D.

Worm gear

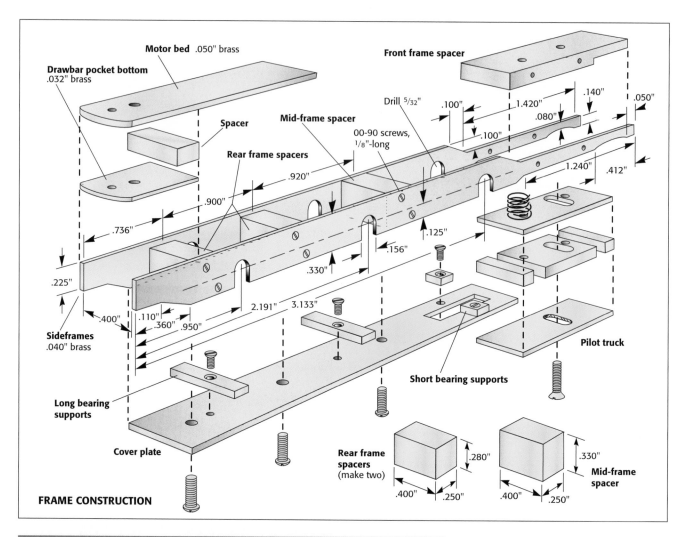

FRAME CONSTRUCTION

Motor bed .050" brass

Drawbar pocket bottom
.032" brass

Spacer

Rear frame spacers

Mid-frame spacer

Front frame spacer

Drill 5/32"

00-90 screws,
1/8"-long

Sideframes
.040" brass

Long bearing
supports

Cover plate

Short bearing supports

Pilot truck

Rear frame
spacers
(make two)

Mid-frame
spacer

.050"
.100"
1.420"
.140"
.080"
.100"
1.240"
.412"
.920"
.900"
.736"
.125"
.156"
.330"
.225"
.400"
.110"
.360"
.950"
2.191"
3.133"
.280"
.400"
.250"
.330"
.400"
.250"

Stephen fabricates the frame from brass bar stock separated by spacer blocks. A brass cover plate holds the driver axles in the frame. All of the frame components are held together by machine screws. The lead truck frame uses similar construction.

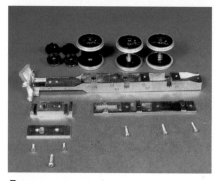

Frame components.

Here's the pilot coupler pocket. File the top of the casting smooth; we'll add details later. File the coupler opening to accept a Kadee pocket.

The cylinder block is made from turned brass cylinders and valve chests surrounded by sheet brass ends and wrapper. These parts are soldered together, see below.

As with all steam locomotives, the side rod holes must match the driver centers exactly. In addition, the main rods, crossheads, and valve gear links should operate smoothly with no binding. Stephen provides templates for all of these parts, which, if followed, will result in a smooth running steam engine.

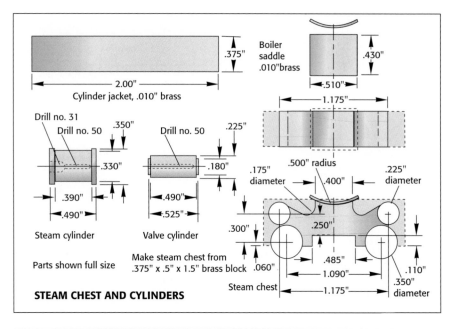

STEAM CHEST AND CYLINDERS

Here Stephen is soldering the cylinders. He holds the steam chest with a clothespin clamped in a vise while soldering the cylinders. The wood clothespin insulates the cylinders from the metal vise, which would act as a large heat sink and keep the parts from heating quickly.

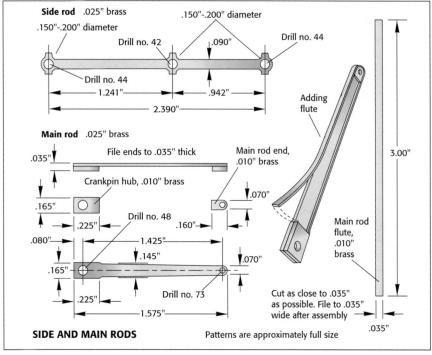

SIDE AND MAIN RODS   Patterns are approximately full size

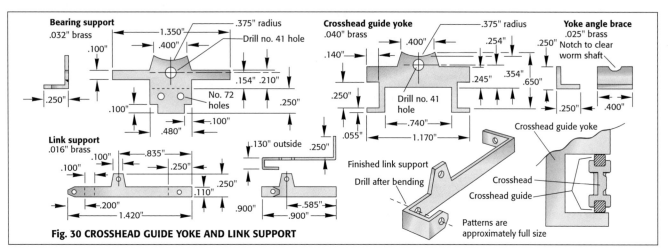

Fig. 30 CROSSHEAD GUIDE YOKE AND LINK SUPPORT

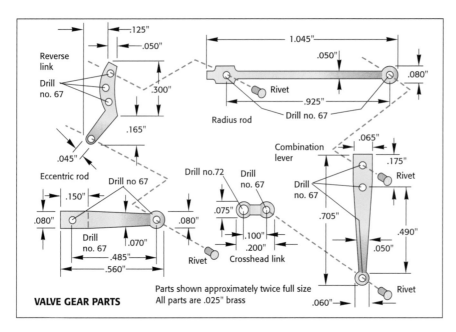

Reverse link
Drill no. 67
.125"
.050"
.300"
.165"
.045"
Eccentric rod
Drill no 67
.150"
.080"
.485"
.560"
.070"
Drill no. 67

Radius rod
1.045"
.050"
.080"
Rivet
.925"
Drill no. 67

Drill no.72
Drill no. 67
.075"
.100"
.200"
Rivet
Crosshead link

Combination lever
.065"
.175"
Rivet
Drill no. 67
.705"
.490"
.050"
Rivet
.060"

VALVE GEAR PARTS
Parts shown approximately twice full size
All parts are .025" brass

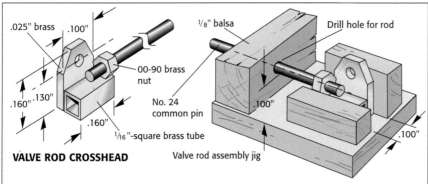

.025" brass
.100"
00-90 brass nut
.160" .130"
.160"
1/16"-square brass tube

1/8" balsa
Drill hole for rod
No. 24 common pin
.100"
Valve rod assembly jig
.100"

VALVE ROD CROSSHEAD

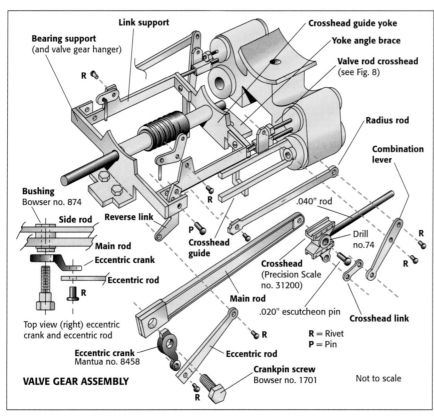

Link support
Bearing support (and valve gear hanger)
Crosshead guide yoke
Yoke angle brace
Valve rod crosshead (see Fig. 8)
R
Radius rod
Combination lever
Bushing Bowser no. 874
Side rod
Reverse link
Main rod
Eccentric crank
Eccentric rod
R
Top view (right) eccentric crank and eccentric rod
P
Crosshead guide
Crosshead (Precision Scale no. 31200)
Main rod
.040" rod
Drill no.74
R
R
.020" escutcheon pin
Crosshead link
R = Rivet
P = Pin
Eccentric crank Mantua no. 8458
Eccentric rod
Crankpin screw Bowser no. 1701
Not to scale
R

VALVE GEAR ASSEMBLY

Two problems in assembling valve gear are handling the small parts and neatly riveting them together. Stephen presents simple solutions, which will work on other locomotives as well as his 4-6-0.

Piece-on-a-stick method

The hardest part of making small parts is simply handling them. Rather than make blanks for parts that are almost the final size, we begin with a long "stick" of brass that's easy to hold. For the valve gear parts, solder two pieces of 1/8" wide .025" brass strip about 6" long together.

Square up the stick, coat it with dye, and lay out the first part, for example, the crosshead link. Drill the holes and file the part to shape. These are small pieces and even with just a file it doesn't take long to make a part. When a part is finished, cut it off the stick with a razor saw or disc cutter and shape the cut end. Unsolder and clean up the new parts.

Now square up the end of the stick and lay out your next part. Before you know it, you'll have all the parts done. Just remember to store them safely.

Riveting

Rivets are not difficult to use if you are careful. Place a rivet head down on a hard surface such as a flat piece of metal. Place the part you want on the outside on the rivet. Over this place the next part, then place a shallow-pointed punch in the end of the rivet and tap lightly with a small hammer, as shown below. This is called "setting" the rivet. You don't need many taps as it only takes a little force to expand the rivet.

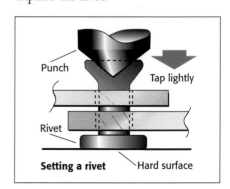

Punch
Tap lightly
Rivet
Setting a rivet
Hard surface

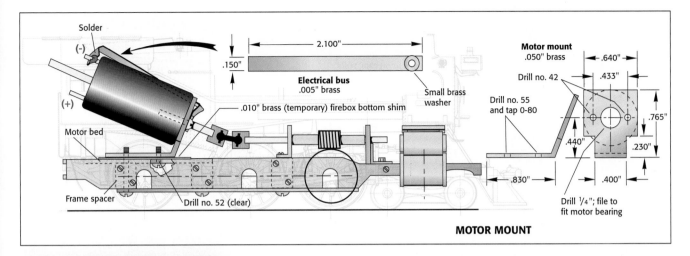

Solder

(-)

(+)

Motor bed

Frame spacer

Drill no. 52 (clear)

Solder to back side

2.100"

.150"

Electrical bus
.005" brass

.010" brass (temporary) firebox bottom shim

Small brass
washer

Motor mount
.050" brass

Drill no. 42

Drill no. 55
and tap 0-80

.640"

.433"

.765"

.440"

.230"

.830"

.400"

Drill ¼"; file to
fit motor bearing

MOTOR MOUNT

With the frame completed (including drivers, rods, valve gear and driver springs installed), it is time to mount the motor, test the mechanism, and add final details. Once this step is finished, Stephen will move on to forming the boiler and firebox.

Even though most modelers have never rolled a steam engine boiler from sheet brass, Stephen provides diagrams (see next page) that make this task straightforward. These methods can be used on other scratchbuilt locomotives, not just the 4-6-0.

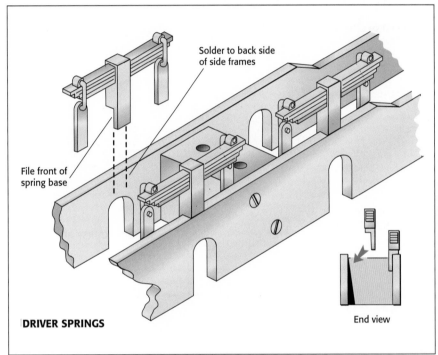

Solder to back side
of side frames

File front of
spring base

End view

DRIVER SPRINGS

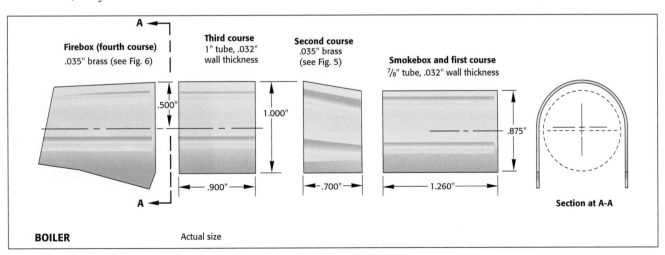

A

Firebox (fourth course)
.035" brass (see Fig. 6)

Third course
1" tube, .032"
wall thickness

Second course
.035" brass
(see Fig. 5)

Smokebox and first course
⁷/₈" tube, .032" wall thickness

.500"

1.000"

.875"

.900"

.700"

1.260"

A

Section at A-A

BOILER

Actual size

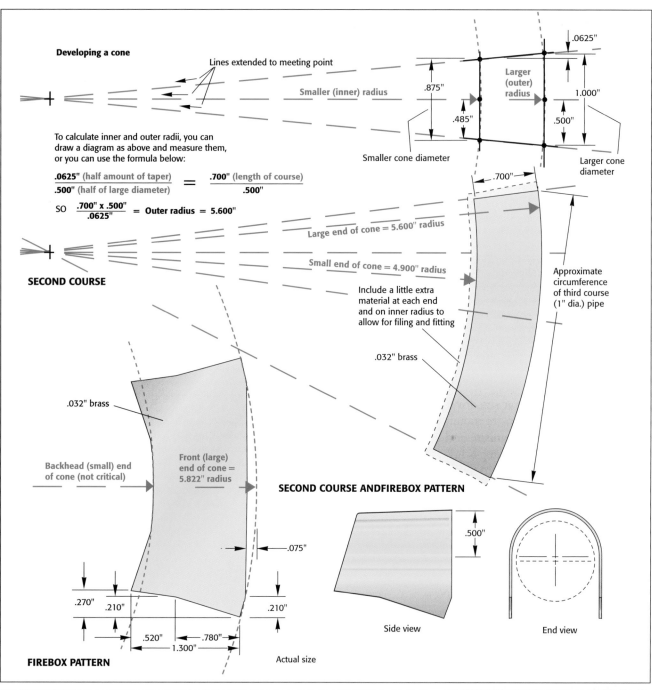

Developing a cone

Lines extended to meeting point

Smaller (inner) radius

.875"

Larger (outer) radius

.0625"

1.000"

.485"

.500"

Smaller cone diameter

Larger cone diameter

To calculate inner and outer radii, you can draw a diagram as above and measure them, or you can use the formula below:

$$\frac{.0625" \text{ (half amount of taper)}}{.500" \text{ (half of large diameter)}} = \frac{.700" \text{ (length of course)}}{.500"}$$

SO $\frac{.700" \times .500"}{.0625"}$ = Outer radius = 5.600"

SECOND COURSE

Large end of cone = 5.600" radius

Small end of cone = 4.900" radius

.700"

Approximate circumference of third course (1" dia.) pipe

Include a little extra material at each end and on inner radius to allow for filing and fitting

.032" brass

SECOND COURSE AND FIREBOX PATTERN

.032" brass

Backhead (small) end of cone (not critical)

Front (large) end of cone = 5.822" radius

.075"

.270"

.210"

.210"

.520"

.780"

1.300"

FIREBOX PATTERN

Actual size

.500"

Side view

End view

FITTING THE SECOND COURSE

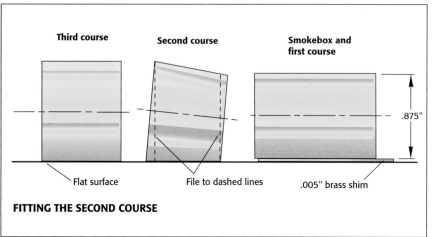

Third course

Second course

Smokebox and first course

.875"

Flat surface

File to dashed lines

.005" brass shim

This is how the finished boiler looks after cleaning up. Don't be upset if, when you finish soldering the sections together, there are globs of solder and flux stains—that's what files and a good washing are for.

With the boiler rolled and assembled, it is time to assemble the ashpan and build the cab.

The assembled ashpan is ready to be mounted below the firebox.

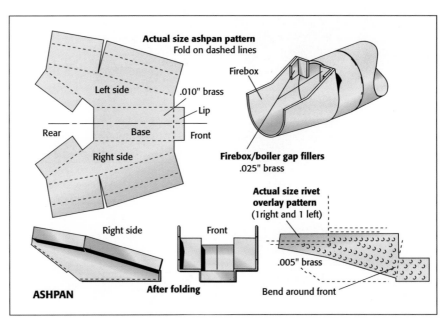

Actual size ashpan pattern
Fold on dashed lines

Left side

.010" brass

Lip

Rear   Base   Front

Right side

Firebox

Firebox/boiler gap fillers
.025" brass

Right side

After folding

Front

Actual size rivet overlay pattern
(1 right and 1 left)

.005" brass

Bend around front

ASHPAN

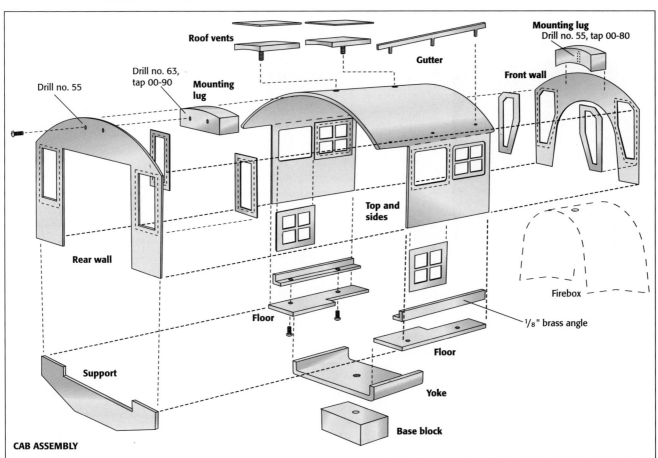

Roof vents

Gutter

Mounting lug
Drill no. 55, tap 00-80

Drill no. 63, tap 00-90   **Mounting lug**

Front wall

Drill no. 55

Top and sides

Rear wall

Firebox

¹⁄₈" brass angle

Floor

Floor

Support

Yoke

Base block

CAB ASSEMBLY

Make a jig to ease cab assembly. Glue a small cube of wood to a 6"-square piece of Masonite or other thin board (such as the wood-paneling scrap shown here). Masonite stands up to repeated gluings and ungluings.

The finished cab is mated to the boiler.

The next step in building the 4-6-0 is to add all of the boiler details: domes, stack, fittings, running boards, etc. Stephen shows his techniques to make the running boards level and the domes centered on top of the boiler.

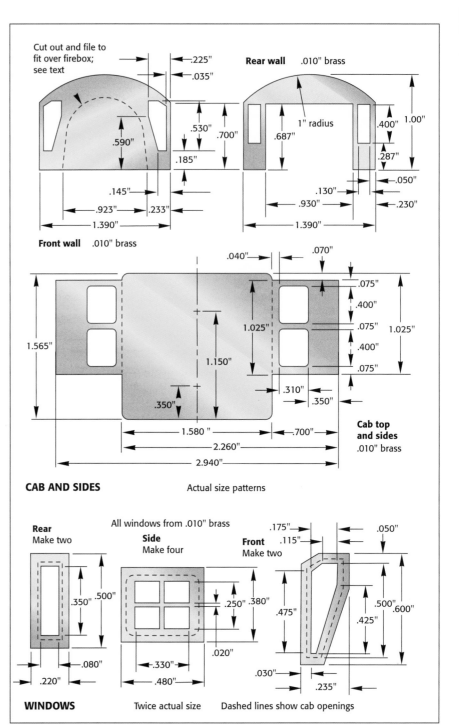

Cut out and file to fit over firebox; see text

Rear wall   .010" brass

.225"
.035"
.530"
.700"
.590"
.185"
.145"
.923"
.233"
1.390"

1" radius
.400"
.687"
1.00"
.287"
.050"
.130"
.930"
.230"
1.390"

Front wall   .010" brass

1.565"
.040"
.070"
.075"
.400"
.075"
1.025"
.400"
.075"
1.025"
1.150"
.350"
.310"
.350"
1.580 "
.700"
2.260"
2.940"

Cab top and sides
.010" brass

CAB AND SIDES   Actual size patterns

All windows from .010" brass

Rear
Make two

Side
Make four

Front
Make two

.350" .500"
.080"
.220"

.250" .380"
.020"
.330"
.480"

.175"
.115"
.050"
.475"
.500" .600"
.425"
.030"
.235"

WINDOWS   Twice actual size   Dashed lines show cab openings

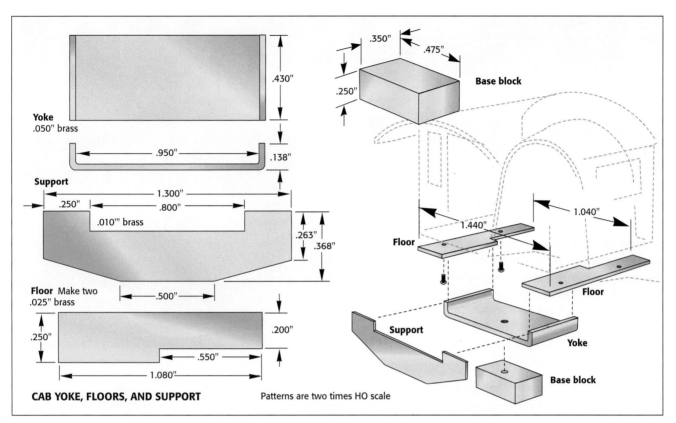

Yoke
.050" brass

.430"

.950"

.138"

Support

1.300"

.250"

.800"

.010''' brass

.263"

.368"

.500"

Floor Make two
.025" brass

.200"

.250"

.550"

1.080"

CAB YOKE, FLOORS, AND SUPPORT   Patterns are two times HO scale

.350"

.475"

.250"

Base block

1.440"

1.040"

Floor

Floor

Support

Yoke

Base block

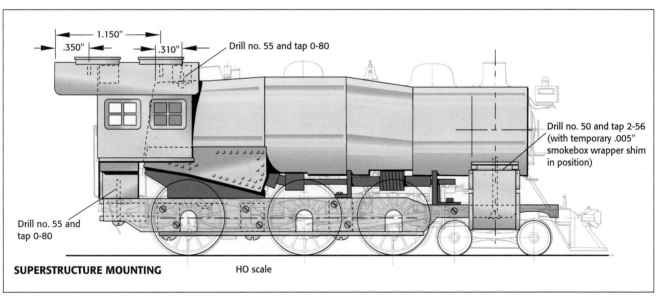

1.150"

.350"

.310"

Drill no. 55 and tap 0-80

Drill no. 50 and tap 2-56
(with temporary .005"
smokebox wrapper shim
in position)

Drill no. 55 and
tap 0-80

SUPERSTRUCTURE MOUNTING   HO scale

55

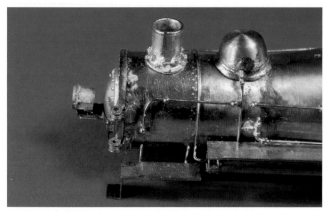

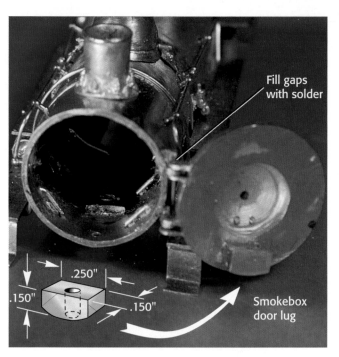

Fill gaps with solder

Smokebox door lug

.250"

.150"

.150"

To fill the gaps between the hinges and smokebox side, first flux the smokebox and the hinge. Then quickly touch a heavily tinned iron to the hinge flange. When cool, file away the excess solder with a square jeweler's file.

To keep the smokebox front closed, make a lug from some scrap brass to the dimension shown. Drill and tap it 00-90, then solder it to the inside. Now drill a no. 55 hole for the screw through the bottom of the smokebox.

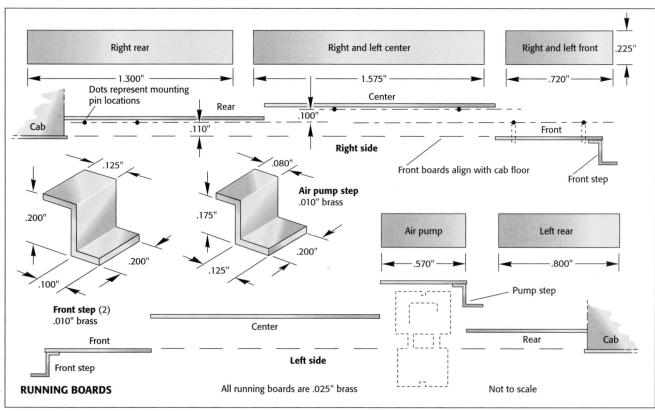

Right rear

Right and left center

Right and left front

.225"

1.300"

1.575"

.720"

Dots represent mounting pin locations

Center

Rear

Cab

.110"

.100"

Right side

Front

Front boards align with cab floor

Front step

.125"

.080"

Air pump step
.010" brass

.200"

.175"

.200"

.200"

.125"

Air pump

Left rear

.100"

.570"

.800"

Front step (2)
.010" brass

Center

Pump step

Front

Rear

Cab

Front step

Left side

RUNNING BOARDS

All running boards are .025" brass

Not to scale

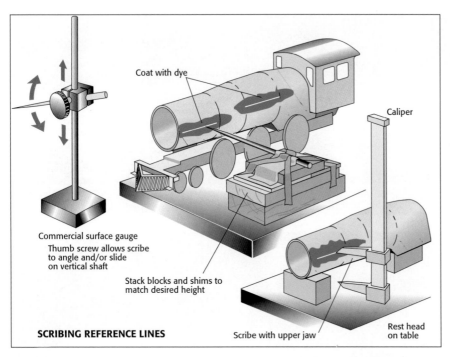

Coat with dye

Caliper

Commercial surface gauge

Thumb screw allows scribe
to angle and/or slide
on vertical shaft

Stack blocks and shims to
match desired height

SCRIBING REFERENCE LINES

Scribe with upper jaw

Rest head
on table

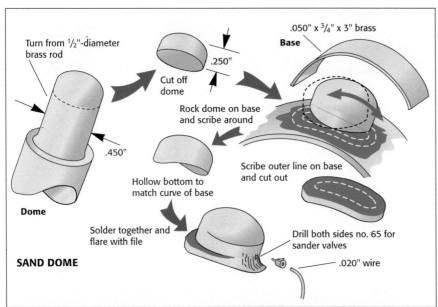

Turn from ¹/₂"-diameter
brass rod

.050" x ³/₄" x 3" brass

Base

Cut off
dome

.250"

Rock dome on base
and scribe around

.450"

Scribe outer line on base
and cut out

Dome

Hollow bottom to
match curve of base

Solder together and
flare with file

Drill both sides no. 65 for
sander valves

.020" wire

SAND DOME

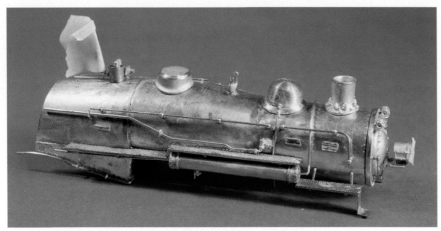

Boiler showing domes, stack, running boards, and details mounted.

Adding the final piping and pilot beam details completes the construction of the 4-6-0. Once painted, the engine will be ready for service on your pike.

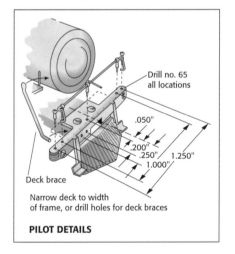

Drill no. 65 all locations

.050"
.200"
.250"
1.000"
1.250"

Deck brace

Narrow deck to width of frame, or drill holes for deck braces

PILOT DETAILS

PAINTING

Prior to 1900, American railroads took pride in the appearance of their steam engines. Dark blue Russia Iron boilers with brass boiler bands and domes often rode on a chassis with red drivers and pilot wheels. These locomotives were kept wiped down and polished by their crews. As locomotives grew larger and rail traffic increased during the first two decades of the twentieth century, there was less time for polish, and coal dust, leaky pipe joints, and ballast dust on the running gear made a steam locomotive look dirty and weather-beaten. The Depression of the 1930s sent many railroads into bankruptcy, and there was no money for new paint, much less polish.

As a degree of prosperity returned in 1938 and the first streamliners appeared, some level of color returned to steam power. While most steam engines were black with a number under the cab window and a roadname on the tender, those assigned to the snappy new passenger colors were again given some spit and polish. The maroon tender panel on Canadian Pacific locomotives, the gunmetal and gray of the New York Central's streamlined Hudsons, and the brilliant red and orange of the Southern Pacific Daylight 4-8-4s, were examples of the railroads giving their passenger motive power an identity to match the new cars they hauled.

World War II, with its heavy rail traffic demands, put an end to the brief re-emergence of color on steam engines. With victory in 1945, a new form of motive power had captured the eyes of railroad management—the diesel electric. As the railroads converted to this new form of motive power, the aging steam engines ran out their final miles looking filthy.

Reproducing the look of a prototype steam engine requires knowing how to paint your model to fit any of these periods. Your new model steam locomotive may come out of the box with crisp factory painting and lettering, but few proto-type engines looked that way more than a few weeks after shopping. This section contains articles that will show you how to paint your model steam locomotive to look like its prototype during the period that you model. *John Pryke*

SIX

Realistic weathering for steam locomotives

Use your airbrush to get that hardworking look

By John Pryke
Model photos by the author

Over the last five years, affordable, highly detailed plastic steam locomotives have led to the reappearance of steam power on many model railroads. Out of the box these models look crisp and clean—quite unlike how their prototypes often appeared.

During the first half of the 20th century when steam was king, most hardworking engines lost their shine soon after being repainted. "Dirty" was the best way to describe them. In the late 1940s and early '50s, the aging steamers ran out their lives with little maintenance and no new paint, as in the photo of the Boston & Albany 2-8-4 on page 61. Here's how to weather your plastic steamers to look like the real thing.

How steam engines "weather"

A steam engine consists of a warm boiler surrounded by water pipes and steam fittings, a hot smokebox in front, and very hot firebox to the rear, all of which rides on a chassis containing many large moving parts. When new, locomotives were painted with shiny black enamel, but in operation each component turned a different color:

• All paint became a grayish-black color from smoke, soot, and the weather, and its shine disappeared.

• The engine's "hot spots"—the smokebox, firebox, and the boiler below the pop (safety) valves and whistle—took on an ash-gray color.

• Water leaks and condensing steam from washout plugs, pop valves, and whistles landed on the boiler, leaving light gray streaks and deposits of scale.

• The expansion and contraction of pipe joints and boiler fittings left rust spots and drip marks.

• The vibration of drivers on the rail kicked up dirt from the roadbed, coating the running gear, trucks, pilot, lower part of the tender, and rear tender beam. The color of this dirt depended on where the locomotive ran.

• Parts subjected to constant wear and rubbing—coupler faces, air hose glad hands, polling pockets, and such—rapidly lost their paint and turned rusty from water hitting the bare metal.

Figure 1 shows this weathering pattern for a typical steam engine.

The tender had its own unique weathering pattern as shown in fig. 2:

• When water was taken on, spills sat in puddles on the tender deck and filler hatch, settled into the crease between the deck and side, and dripped down the side, often following vertical rivet lines. Rust formed as paint wore off and the water dried.

An Athearn USRA light 2-8-2, weathered and lettered as a New York Central H-6a, rumbles into a yard on author John Pryke's HO layout. The year is 1949, and John's weathering makes this model look like it's 30 years old.

• Dirt kicked up by the engine coated the trucks and lower sides of the body.

• Broad, light gray streaks often appeared on the sides of the tender from steam condensing and leaving a deposit of scale.

The box on page 65 lists model paints that match these colors and shows how to alter the dirt color to match different regions.

Getting started

I apply most of the weathering on a steam model with an airbrush, although I paint small details with a 5/0 paintbrush. With my Badger no. 150 dual-action airbrush, I use a medium tip for the base coat and a fine tip for details.

If you use Polly Scale colors, dilute them 20-25 percent with distilled water (available at most drug stores). Floquil colors should be diluted 15-20 percent with Dio-Sol thinner. Test Floquil paint on the inside of the tender shell to make sure it will not attack the plastic.

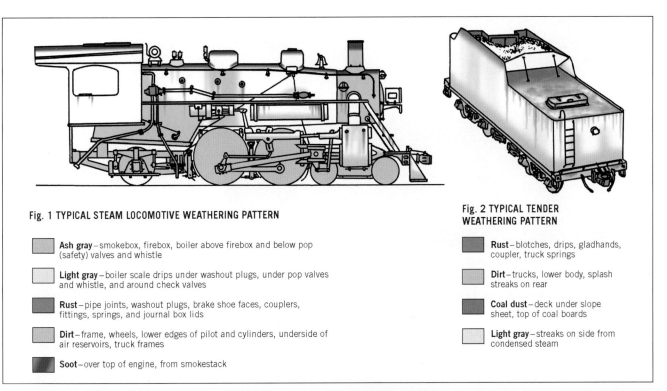

Fig. 1 TYPICAL STEAM LOCOMOTIVE WEATHERING PATTERN

Fig. 2 TYPICAL TENDER WEATHERING PATTERN

Ash gray—smokebox, firebox, boiler above firebox and below pop (safety) valves and whistle

Light gray—boiler scale drips under washout plugs, under pop valves and whistle, and around check valves

Rust—pipe joints, washout plugs, brake shoe faces, couplers, fittings, springs, and journal box lids

Dirt—frame, wheels, lower edges of pilot and cylinders, underside of air reservoirs, truck frames

Soot—over top of engine, from smokestack

Rust—blotches, drips, gladhands, coupler, truck springs

Dirt—trucks, lower body, splash streaks on rear

Coal dust—deck under slope sheet, top of coal boards

Light gray—streaks on side from condensed steam

Stephen Payne

(Above) It's January 1949 and *cold* as Boston & Albany 2-8-4 no. 1449 releases steam from her safety valves as she waits to leave Worcester, Mass. (Left) Fig. 3 With clip leads attached to the locomotive, John rotates the drivers slowly to apply the Grimy Black base coat evenly to the drivers, rods, and valve gear. This method of painting the running gear avoids time-consuming and potentially troublesome disassembly.

When airbrushing, I wear disposable latex gloves. They allow me to hold the parts without getting paint all over my hands, so I don't have to wipe my skin with thinner to remove paint.

I recently painted an Athearn Genesis United States Railroad Administration light 2-8-2, typical of the new breed of plastic steam. It came with the footboard pilot and centered headlight appropriate for the New York Central's class H-6a Mikados.

The NYC received 194 USRA light 2-8-2s, and their appearance changed little during their long service. They were among the last steamers scrapped by the NYC, and I painted my model to look as it would have during the

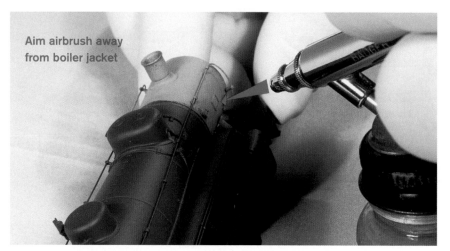

Aim airbrush away from boiler jacket

Fig. 4 When painting the smokebox, John aims the nozzle of the airbrush forward and away from the boiler (the boiler actually begins at the rear of the smokebox). With a little practice, even small areas of different color can be painted by careful aiming.

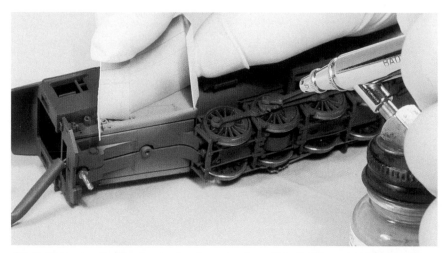

Fig. 5 John uses baffles to mask adjacent colors. This baffle was cut from an index card and bent to the shape of the firebox. John holds it in place while the firebox is being sprayed ash gray to protect the Grimy Black cab, drivers, and running board.

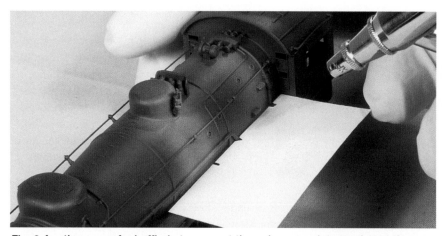

Fig. 6 Another use of a baffle is to prevent the ash gray paint streaks on the boiler from getting on the Grimy Black running boards. This baffle fits snugly against the boiler on top of the running board, and John cut notches to clear cast-on piping.

railraod's transition to diesel power.

Prior to painting, I installed the engine's handrails as well as the tender marker lights, ladder, air hose, and rear coupler per instructions. I didn't install the locomotive's classification lights until after painting.

I then disassembled the model, removing the leading and trailing trucks, the injector pipes on both sides of the firebox, and the four air pipes under the right-hand running board. The pipes can be pried loose from their mountings with a small screwdriver.

I removed the smokebox front, unplugging the headlight LED and setting it aside. I gently pulled the headlight out of the smokebox (it's a press fit) and put small pieces of masking tape over its front and rear to keep paint off the lens.

The front running boards and ladders can be removed by prying their pins out of the holes in the pilot deck and snapping them off the cylinder pipes.

Removing the cab and boiler from the chassis takes a lot of force, so I decided to leave them in place. Tender disassembly included removing the shell, trucks, and floor. Finally, I applied Micro-Mask liquid masker to all of the wheel treads and allowed it to dry overnight.

The weathering process

The box on the opposite page lists the different steps required to weather a steam engine. I started by spraying all locomotive and tender components with a base coat of Polly Scale Grimy Black using the medium tip in my airbrush. To give the drivers and rods an even finish, I attached clip leads to the drawbar pin and the opposite side of the split frame under the pilot deck. With the clip leads connected to a power pack, I slowly rotated the drivers as I sprayed them, as shown in fig. 3 on page 61.

After completing the base coat, I cleaned my airbrush by spraying Badger Airbrush Cleaner through it. I then disassembled it and cleaned each component. I clean my airbrush whenever I change colors so dried paint won't build up. A clean airbrush is essential for a good paint job. After switching to the fine tip I added the weathering details.

Aiming and baffles

I started by spraying the smokebox ash gray. I held my airbrush over the boiler and aimed the spray forward at the smokebox to keep the gray off the black cylinders and boiler (see fig. 4). With practice you can achieve a clean separation between the two colors.

The running boards, cab front, and drivers surround the firebox. To protect the Grimy Black of these parts while painting the firebox ash gray, I used a baffle—a paint shield cut from a 3 x 5 index card. It's handy for painting different colors in tight quarters.

I bent the baffle to match the outline of the firebox and held it in place (see fig. 5) while spraying ash gray. When I removed the baffle, only the firebox was gray and the other parts remained black.

Next, I added some ash gray to the boiler below the steam dome and above the firebox. I made a second baffle to fit on top of the running board with its edge tight against the boiler. I cut small notches in it to clear the boiler's cast-on piping (see fig. 6).

Making a drip stencil

To add scale and rust "drips" to the boiler under washout plugs, pop valves, and the whistle, I use a drip stencil made from a 3 x 5 index card as shown in fig. 7a. One stencil card can contain all the different patterns I use. I lay the stencil on the engine and spray through it to paint neat drip lines.

Figure 7b shows how I sprayed light gray (for boiler scale) through the stencil onto the boiler to create a drip below a washout plug. Neat drip lines remain after the stencil is removed, as in fig. 7c.

The drip stencil is a versatile tool. You can spray through either side for "mirror image" drips, or overlay different patterns for variation. You can spray

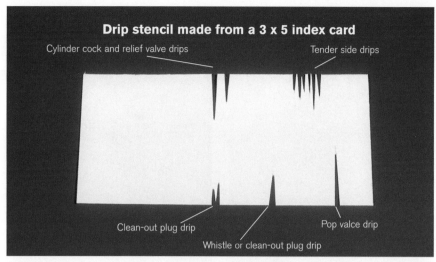

Drip stencil made from a 3 x 5 index card

Cylinder cock and relief valve drips

Tender side drips

Clean-out plug drip

Whistle or clean-out plug drip

Pop valce drip

Fig. 7a You can make one stencil for all the drip patterns on both a locomotive and tender. John made this one by cutting V-shaped notches into the edges of an index card.

Fig. 7b Here John shows how he uses the stencil card to paint drip lines from boiler washout plugs and fittings. He positions the stencil pattern he wants over the fitting to be weathered and sprays through the stencil onto the boiler or other surface.

Fig. 7c After using the stencil, distinct drip marks remain on the locomotive's boiler.

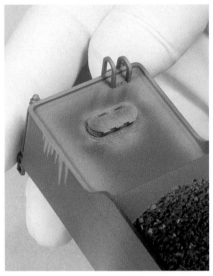

Fig. 8 To make the deck of the tender rusty, John aimed his airbrush so excess paint shot away from the side. He used the drip stencil to paint rusty overflow streaks left when taking water.

Fig. 9 Again John used clip leads connected to a power pack to rotate the drivers slowly while spraying on the dirt coating. This ensures even coverage, and keeps the rods from masking the drivers and leaving unrealistic grimy black stripes.

Steps in the weathering process

1. Apply the base coat to locomotive and tender.
2. Paint smokebox, firebox, and boiler (under pop valves, whistle, and above firebox).
3. Add drip marks to cylinder cocks and boiler washout plugs, pop valves, and whistle.
4. Add rust on tender deck and side drips.
5. Hand-paint handrails, cast-on piping, and running boards with base coat over weathering.
6. Hand-paint rust on pipe joints, truck springs, journal lids, and rerail frogs.
7. Reassemble locomotive and tender.
8. Spray dirt on chassis and trucks.
9. Apply decals or dry transfers.
10. Spray Dullcote from airbrush on decals (only).
11. Apply control coat to mute weathering.
12. Apply light coat of soot over top of engine.
13. Hand-paint fresh rust on coupler faces, glad hands, and brake shoe faces.

one color, rust for example, then move the stencil slightly to one side and spray a second color, such as light gray.

Washout plugs not properly tightened often left a rusty drip when the locomotive was shopped and continued leaking when it was back in service, leaving a scaly drip over the rust. To complete the locomotive's weathering, I added a round leak from water oozing out of a check valve by a quick, small spray of light gray just behind the valve. This can be seen below the sand dome.

Weathering the tender

I started with the tender deck. First I aimed a spray of Rust to hit the seam between the deck and side from inboard, so the overspray went over the outside wall as in fig. 8. I slowly rotated the tender to spray the entire seam. I added blotches of rust to the deck, with a heavier coating on the filler hatch. Using the stencil, I painted rusty water drips on the side and back of the tank just below the top beading. I also sprayed two or three light vertical bands of ash gray on each side to simulate scale deposits left by condensing steam.

Dirt coating on chassis and trucks

A steamer's pounding action on the track coats the running gear with dirt. Before adding this coating, I reassembled the engine and tender. For my NYC 2-8-2 that runs in the East, I used a coating of Polly Scale Earth. I again hooked up clip leads as in fig. 9, and rotated the drivers as I sprayed for even coverage of the wheels and rods.

After removing the clip leads, I sprayed dirt on the rest of the chassis. The coating extends about 1/4" up the side of the tender, as dust and dirt usually shot several feet into the air. I also painted the bottom of the cylinders and pilot steps. I added two vertical streaks on the rear tender wall, above the rails, to simulate dirt thrown up by the wheels of the car just behind.

Touchup with a fine paintbrush

At this point some details, such as piping and handrails, have been painted the same color as the boiler streaks and smokebox. Parts mounted away from the surface should retain their original black color, albeit grimy. I repainted these parts with a 5/0 pointed-tip brush as shown in fig. 10 on page 66. I also highlighted the tender truck springs, journal lids, and rerail frogs with rust.

Decals

I lettered my locomotive and tender with Microscale no. 87-78 New York Central Steam Engine decals. I applied a coat of Solvaset over each decal to make it snuggle down over raised details and let them dry overnight. I then oversprayed the decals with Dullcote from my airbrush to hide their shine.

[Most decal makers advise applying decals over a clear gloss coat. Modelers then use a clear flat spray to both seal the decals and dull the finish. —Ed.]

The control coat

At this point the model still looks garish and unrealistic. The key step is to apply a control coat of thinned grimy black to mute the weathering and obtain the exact finish you want. The more control coat applied, the more muted the weathering becomes.

The two Athearn 2-8-2s in fig. 11 show the effect of a control coat. The locomotive at the top has no control coat and appears over-weathered. A control coat has been applied to the other, and it looks much more realistic. As a rule of thumb, freight engines were left to the elements and the weathering was very prominent. Passenger engines were regularly wiped down and looked somewhat cleaner.

For your first weathering projects, make your control coat by thinning whatever grimy black paint you use by 50 percent with distilled water (for acrylics) or Dio-Sol (for solvent-based paints). This dilution may require a few more passes with the airbrush, but you won't accidentally erase your weathering. As you gain experience, you can reduce the amount of thinner.

Before applying the control coat, be sure to mask any clear parts that are to remain shiny, such as headlight lenses and cab window glazing.

I sprayed a light control coat evenly over the entire locomotive and tender, including the decals. I left the weathering quite prominent to make my engine look like a well-used freight hog during the transition period.

Paint for weathering steam locomotives

Locomotive color: Base coat
Polly Scale (water-based acrylic): Grimy Black
Floquil (enamel thinned with organic solvents): Grimy Black

Locomotive color: Ash gray—firebox, smokebox, and boiler under pop (safety) valves and whistle and above firebox
Polly Scale: Erie Lackawanna Gray
Floquil: Grime

Locomotive color: Light gray—boiler scale, drips from fittings
Polly Scale: D&H Gray
Floquil: Gray Primer

Locomotive color: Rust—drips, blotches
Polly Scale: Rust
Floquil: Rust

Locomotive color: Dirt coating—on cylinders, engine and tender running gear, rear tender streaks
Polly Scale: Various, see below
Floquil: Various, see below

Locomotive color: Control coat
Polly Scale: Grimy Black, thinned 50 percent with distilled water
Floquil: thinned 50 percent with Dio-Sol

Locomotive color: Soot and cinders
Polly Scale: Engine Black
Floquil: Engine Black

Locomotive color: Coal—in tender
Polly Scale: Engine Black
Floquil: Engine Black

Locomotive color: Oil—on filler caps and drips on tender (for oil-burning locomotives only)
Polly Scale: Oily Black
Floquil: No match in this line, use Polly Scale Oily Black

Dirt color mixes for different regions

Region: Northeast
Polly Scale: Earth
Floquil: Earth

Region: Southeast
Polly Scale: 3 parts Earth, 1 part Oxide Red
Floquil: 3 parts Earth, 1 part Boxcar Red

Region: Midwest
Polly Scale: 3 parts Earth, 1 part Mud
Floquil: 3 parts Earth, 1 part Mud

Region: Mountain states
Polly Scale: 3 parts Earth, 2 parts MOW Gray
Floquil: 3 parts Earth, 2 parts Grime

Region: Desert Southwest
Polly Scale: Dust
Floquil: Dust

Region: Northwest
Polly Scale: Dirt
Floquil: 3 parts Earth, 1 part Roof Brown

Final details

I sprayed a light coat of Engine Black over the top of the engine from above. This simulates cinders and soot from the smokestack settling on the top of the boiler, cab, and tender. Apply only enough to suit the type of railroad you model. On a railroad with many grades, a steam engine will work hard going uphill and throw off lots of soot and cinders in billows of smoke. On a relatively flat line, the locomotive works mainly to start and accelerate a train, and thus

produces much less soot. I then added fresh Rust to the couplers, brake shoe faces, and air hose glad hands with a 5/0 brush.

I painted the cast coal load in the tender engine black, using a brush to get into the corners. To add realism, I poured a little Woodland Scenics coal into an old pill bottle, added a few drops of the same maker's Scenic Cement, and mixed them together. Using tweezers, I put some lumps of coal onto the tender deck, just behind the slope sheet. When these had

dried, I brushed Scenic Cement onto the cast coal load and onto the tender deck around the lumps of coal, then sprinkled a very light coat of Highball Products coal dust over the wet cement. This gave the cast coal load a realistic sheen.

With the painting complete, I peeled the Micro Mask off the wheel treads using a no. 17 blade. Next I put the engine and tender on a test track and made sure they ran smoothly. At last I coupled the Mike to a train and put it to work on my railroad.

Fig. 10 Several parts, including handrails, cast-on pipes, and some fittings have been sprayed the color of the smokebox or firebox behind them. The easiest way to return them to their original Grimy Black is by hand-painting with a very fine brush.

Fig. 11 Control coat is the key to John's technique. The engine at the top has the stark look of only the basic weathering. The other locomotive shows how the control coat mutes and blends the colors realistically.

SEVEN A South Park Cooke Mogul in Sn3

A steam locomotive paint job that goes beyond basic black

By David Steer
Photos by the author

In this article I'll show how I painted an Sn3 model of one of these colorful locomotives. Although the details of this article are specific to South Park locomotives, the techniques and processes are applicable to any locomotive of the same era.

This model belongs to a fellow South Park modeler in Europe. After rebuilding the engine to resemble no. 71, he sent it to a friend of mine on this side of the Atlantic for detailing and painting. Eventually, my friend got so busy he was unable to finish the locomotive. That's when I stepped in.

The Denver, South Park & Pacific's Moguls were certainly colorful locomotives. Here David Steer describes how he painted this Sn3 brass model of no. 71.

Rebuilding

Overland's Colorado & Southern no. 21 is a good starting point for conversion. The tender has the characteristic flared top flange and the boiler and drivers are also correct. Since I only completed the conversion and painted the model, I can't take complete credit. But I will briefly describe the modifications made by the locomotive's owner.

Starting with the tender, he modified the trucks for outside hung brake beams, added dual air tanks on the rear deck, and removed the coal board extensions from the tank top. That's where I took over. I assembled the South Park Finescale toolboxes and set them aside until after painting. Next, I installed Precision Scale water valves on the front of the tank and added a brake staff to the fireman's side of the tender.

I removed the Overland brake cylinders since early Cookes had smaller cylinders. I also replaced the pilot with a Berlyn Locomotive Works South Park casting. A new pilot truck bearing, turned on a lathe, was applied to the deck. Finally, I added a long coupler link and air hose.

The boiler received the most extensive alteration. After removing the headlight, stack, air tanks, bell, domes, air pump, running boards, and cab, I shortened the smokebox by cutting along the line of rivets in the middle, removing the extended smokebox. The headlight bracket is from Precision Scale (PSC), topped with a Berlyn South Park oil headlight. The Congdon stack is also from Berlyn. I also replaced the steel running boards with simulated wooden ones. Finally, I installed a new steam and sand dome from South Park Finescale.

I replaced the Overland cab with an etched brass one from South Park Finescale, soldering the sides and rear together to match the front of the Overland model. Then I added brass angle, drilling and tapping holes so the cab could be screwed securely to the frame.

I replaced the modern appliances on the boiler backhead with vintage ones. The steam turret, throttle, air and steam gauges, Johnson bar, and air brake stand are all from PSC. The water glass was removed as the early Cookes were fitted with tri-cocks on the back of the boiler. The result is a sparse-looking cab that captures the look of 19th-century locomotives.

Disassembly and cleaning

When painting a multicolored model, it's best to disassemble as much as possible. Like most imported brass models, this one had a clear protective coating that I removed prior to painting, using Scalecoat paint remover in an ultrasonic cleaner.

After all the modifications, the model was covered with flux and filings. To clean the surface completely, I used a solvent designed for cleaning printed-circuit boards. This solvent is available from most electronics supply stores or mail order catalogs. It dissolves the flux, leaving a clean, grease-free surface. To remove heavy tarnish, I use Tarn-X, a chemical cleaner available in the hardware store. Dishwashing detergent in water will also clean a model, although it may take a little longer. Use distilled water for rinsing as tap water often contains dissolved minerals, which can leave water spots on the model. I dried the model with compressed air.

Avoid touching the clean model

Here's the disassembled model ready for painting. Note how Dave mounts the various subassemblies on long toothpicks to make for easier handling when painting.

The boiler has already been painted Russia Iron and then carefully masked so the cab front can be painted Tuscan Red. Once the red has dried, David will mask it and spray the running boards, smokebox, and headlight black.

with your bare hands because finger oil can affect paint adhesion. All this may seem like a lot of work, but good preparation is the most basic step to getting a fine finish on the model.

Masking

I elected to finish this model with polished brass boiler bands, commonly found on locomotives of the period. Since nothing simulates polished brass like polished brass, I polished the bands before painting the model by applying a small amount of Brasso polish and buffing with Q-Tips.

I masked the bands with Scotch magic transparent tape. I applied this tape over the boiler bands in wide strips and trimmed it to width by running a sharp hobby knife along the edge of the band.

I also masked the wheel treads using Scotch no. 471 flexible ⅛"-wide plastic automobile striping tape. This tape can be stretched around the driver tread and the flange. Finally, I used ordinary masking tape to completely cover the inside bearings.

Painting

Once the basic masking is completed, the various subassemblies can be painted. I use large toothpicks as handles during painting, preferring them because they are disposable and can be stuck into a scrap of foam board while the paint dries.

I used Scalecoat paints, thinning them 7 parts paint to 3 parts thinner. These are too glossy for a finished model, but since real locomotives were painted with gloss paint I feel models should be the same before weathering. Without an underlying gloss finish it's hard to duplicate the contrast of clean and dirty areas on the prototype.

I started by applying my Russia Iron, described in the sidebar, to the boiler jacket. After this had dried for about a week, I masked the jacket and sprayed the front of the cab Tuscan Red. After that had dried, I masked the cab front and airbrushed the remainder of the boiler, smokebox, and backhead black.

The front of the prototype cab was wood (see sidebar) with a metal plate attached to the boiler and firebox. This was usually painted black, and I masked the front of the cab to leave a black rectangle that simulates this.

The cab interior, underside of the

Period colors and paint mixes

I finished this model to match the builder's photo of DSP&P no. 71. The 1884 photo is black-and-white, so the first task was deciding on appropriate colors. I developed a color scheme from studying the builder's photo and reviewing colors used on other locomotives of the same era.

Here's my color scheme:

Boiler jacket—Russia Iron. This is an iron sheet specially treated so it will not rust. It's generally a steel gray color, with a bluish cast caused by the reflection from the sky. My preferred mix for Russia Iron is 6 parts Floquil Gunmetal and 4 parts Floquil Dark Gray.

Boiler bands—brass.
Handrails and brackets—brass.
Bell—brass.
Bell bracket—black.
Smoke box, stack, domes, head- light, air pump, running boards, firebox, and boiler backhead—black.

Frame and pilot—black with white tires on drivers and pilot wheels. The nickel silver rods were left unpainted and were later coated with molybdenum sulfide (NeoLube) to simulate steel.

Cab—varnished wood with canvas roof. I used Tuscan Red to simulate mahogany or cherry. I used Tamiya Buff for the cab window frames to simulate honey oak. The cab roof is painted gray to simulate canvas.

Tender—black with white tires on the wheels. I painted the toolboxes on each side of the coal pocket brown to represent varnished wood.

Lettering—gold with red drop shadows. Gold filigree striping on the domes and headlight.

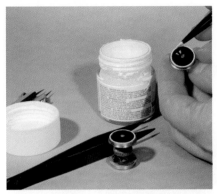

David uses a ruling pen and paint to stripe the tires. The trick is loading enough paint to complete the tire without stopping.

A set of dividers ensures the lettering is even and straight before burnishing. Hold the dry transfer in place with a bit of tape.

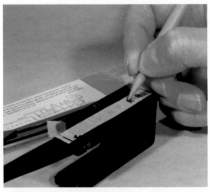

The lettering is burnished onto the surface of the model using an HB pencil. David makes sure he covers all the letters completely.

cab roof, and exterior window frames were then painted Tamiya Buff to represent varnished oak. After this dried, I carefully masked the cab interior and window frames and painted the exterior of the cab Tuscan Red. Finally, I sprayed the cab roof gray.

I used a ruling pen to apply Tamiya White to the tires. I first adjusted the pen for the appropriate width, dipped the nub in the paint, and rotated the wheelset by hand as I striped the wheel. I created an even line by catching one half of the tip on the edge of the tire. Be sure to fill the ruling pen with enough paint for a complete stripe, as stopping to reload the pen in mid wheel will produce uneven widths.

Reassembly and detail painting

After the paint had dried completely (at least 48 hours), I reassembled the model. It's critical that all paint that may interfere with electrical contact be removed prior to putting the locomotive back together. Small parts, such as the bell and handrails, are attached with cyanoacrylate adhesive (CA).

Using a small brush and Tamiya acrylics I painted the air hoses brown. Then I painted the valve handles brass with red centers. The brake shoes are silver. Tiny dabs of silver paint were also applied to the mating surfaces of the air hose glad hands and the piston rod in the center of the air pump.

Inside the cab I painted the gauge faces white. The knobs, levers, and handles are highlighted with brass and red. After the gauge faces dried, I trimmed the edges with brass and carefully touched the gauge faces with black to represent the digits and the needle on the dials. I painted the seat covers and cab floor boards brown. To simulate wear I drybrushed the ratchets for the throttle and Johnson bar with brass. The model was now ready for lettering.

Drop shadow lettering

Dry-transfer lettering for early South Park locomotives is available in HO, S, O, and G scales from CDS Lettering as set no. 703.

Proper positioning is the most important step when applying dry transfers. I cut out the transfer and positioned it on the model. Next, I checked alignment with dividers, measuring from the edge of the model to be sure everything was straight. Then I taped the sheet in

---

Bill of materials

Berlyn Locomotive Works
P. O. Box 9766
Denver, CO 80209
DSP&P oil headlight
Congdon stack
DSP&P pilot

CDS Lettering
S-703 DSP&P locomotives

Floquil
110108 Gunmetal
110132 Dark Gray

Polly Scale
404103 Satin Clear Finish
assorted weathering colors

Precision Scale
headlight bracket
cab interior parts (various)

Scalecoat
10 Black
21 Brown
68 Gray
69 Tuscan Red

South Park Finescale
8 Hendrie Court
Kanata, Ontario, Canada K2L 4A4
DSP&P cab
DSP&P domes
tender toolboxes

Tamiya
81011 Silver
81301 Black
81302 White
81357 Buff

place and burnished the transfer with an HB medium blunt pencil. I rubbed each letter completely and removed the transfer paper. If any part of the lettering didn't transfer, I repositioned the paper and burnished again. I applied the gold lettering first and followed it with the red shadow.

After the letters were transferred, I placed the plain backing sheet over the lettering and burnished once more to set the transfer on the model. I added gold scroll work using an old set of Sloan HO scale old-time passenger car decals.

The CDS transfer set includes the front number plate. I painted a disk of brass black and applied the transfer number to it. The builder's plates are from South Park Finescale.

Here's a broadside view of the engineer's side of the completed locomotive posed to match the Cooke 1884 builder's photo.

Final finish

I removed the masking from the boiler bands and sprayed the locomotive with Polly Scale Satin Clear Finish.

Next, I added some very light weathering with heavily diluted oversprays of Polly Scale Dust, Mud, and Gray to highlight the details.

I cut the cab window glass from microscope slide covers using a carbide scriber. After the glass was cut to size, I secured it in place with white glue.

Some crewmen and a coal load, and this South Park Mogul is ready to head for Alpine Tunnel.

Careful attention to the fine detail inside the cab adds a dash of color and a great deal of character to the completed model.

MAINTENANCE
and Performance

Like its prototype, a model steam engine must be properly maintained to give continuing good performance on your layout. Luckily, the modeler does not have to clean out boiler tubes or turn wheels with flat spots. However, you must know the best way to clean wheels for good electric pickup, where to put oil and grease, and what kind of oil and grease to use.

As parts wear, however, mere cleaning and lubrication are not enough. Knowing how to replace bearings, shafts, and even gears and gearboxes are part of keeping model locomotives in top running condition. Much of the work is straightforward, but some of the techniques and tools may be new.

The articles in this section cover the required annual maintenance as well as techniques to achieve better performance from your locomotives. While a model steam locomotive may run smoothly when it is new, the authors of these articles will describe their techniques to keep it running that way for many years to come. *John Pryke*

EIGHT

Tune up your steam locomotives

Routine maintenance to keep your engines running smoothly

By John Pryke
Photos by the author

During the past few years, we've been fortunate to have several new steam locomotives released in plastic. While these high-quality plastic engines arrive from the factory with their running gears clean and lubricated, over time their drivers and wheels pick up dirt from the track, causing poor electrical contact. Wheel cleaning and periodic lubrication are critical to keep their moving parts operating smoothly. By developing and following a routine maintenance schedule, you can get years of dependable service from these engines on your layout.

Service cycle

How frequently you should service your plastic steam locomotives depends on how often you run them. For example, I hold monthly, three-hour-long operating sessions during nine months of the year and run trains between these sessions. With that frequency of operation, I clean the wheels of each locomotive at the start of the operating season and lubricate each of my engines about once every two years.

If you don't run your engines on a specific schedule, you can usually tell when they need servicing based on their performance. Locomotives that run with a jerky motion or stop and must be pushed to get started need their wheels cleaned. Engines drawing more current than usual and slowing down need lubrication. And if the gear train sounds noisy, it needs oil or grease.

Servicing steam locomotives

The first step in maintaining a locomotive is to clean all the parts that conduct electricity: locomotive drivers, tender wheels, and any electrical wipers that rub against the wheels. The accompanying photos offer techniques you can use to clean the current conductors on your own locomotives. These parts are easy to clean because you don't need to disassemble the locomotive. To lubricate the gear train and bearings, however, you will need to take apart your engine. I've provided instructions for disassembling plastic steam locomotives on page 75.

Lubricants

Lubricating a plastic steam locomotive with quality, plastic-compatible oil and grease is essential for smooth performance and years of good operation. I use Labelle lubricants specifically designed for use on models. The lubricants are offered in different types and viscosities. The table on page 74 lists the recommended uses for each type.

Depending on how often you run your locomotives, you may be surprised at how infrequently they need servicing. Labelle lubricants last a long time, so you may need to lubricate your engines only once every couple of years.

Reassembly and final testing

After the locomotive is lubricated and reassembled, wipe any excess lubricant off the paint. Then place the engine on its back in the cradle and apply power, using either clip leads or the wiper used on the driver treads to clean the locomotive wheels. Make sure the mechanism turns easily and runs smoothly. This is also a good time to touch up any paint that may have chipped off while the engine was being serviced.

It's good practice to give the locomotive a test run once you've finished your maintenance routine. If possible, use a track powered through an ammeter so you can keep an eye on the amount of current the engine draws and to make sure there are no shorts. Periodic maintenance pays dividends in smooth operation and long engine life.

Step 1 Preparing engines for maintenance

Start by placing the engine on its back in a foam cradle with its drivers up. If the engine uses its drawbar to conduct electricity from the tender to the engine, attach one clip lead from your power source to the drawbar and the other to a metal portion of the chassis. If your locomotive picks up only from the drivers, you can build a simple wheel wiper using styrene and brass. The illustration below shows how to make one.

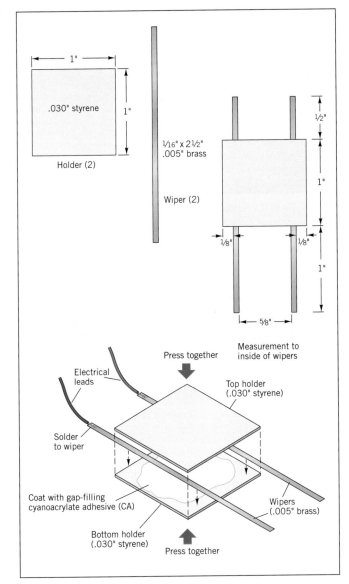

1"

1"

.030" styrene

1"

Holder (2)

1/16" x 2 1/2"
.005" brass

Wiper (2)

1/2"

1"

1/8"   1/8"

1"

5/8"

Measurement to inside of wipers

Press together

Electrical leads

Top holder (.030" styrene)

Solder to wiper

Coat with gap-filling cyanoacrylate adhesive (CA)

Wipers (.005" brass)

Bottom holder (.030" styrene)

Press together

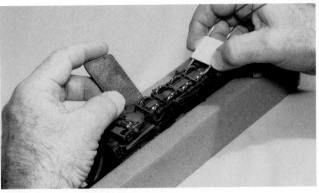

Step 2 Cleaning wheels

There are two ways to remove dirt from the driver treads. The first is with abrasives. Start by cutting one edge of a track-cleaning block, such as a Bright Boy, so it forms a 90-degree angle. Then, with the power wiper in one hand (making sure the contacts are touching both driver treads), apply enough power to turn the drivers at medium speed. (You can also use the clip leads shown in step 1.) With the wheels rotating, press the abrasive block so that the 90-degree corner rides along the radius between the tire tread and the flange. Keep the block in this position until the entire driver tread is clean.

An alternative method for cleaning drivers is to use a liquid solvent that dissolves and lifts off the dirt. A popular product used by modelers is Goo Gone. With the drivers rotating, dip a Q-tip or small cotton swab in Goo Gone and apply it directly to the wheel treads. When the treads appear to be clean, run a dry cotton swab or Q-tip over the tire.

The only drawback to using Goo Gone is that it leaves an oily residue on the drivers. While this residue conducts electricity, it also gets on the track and can decrease a locomotive's traction. If you have grades on your layout greater than 1 percent, but still want to use a liquid solvent to clean wheels, you may want to use other cleaners such as Craftsman Specialty Supply's No-Ox and Micro-Mark's Wheel and Track Cleaner. These products will get the wheels clean without the oily residue.

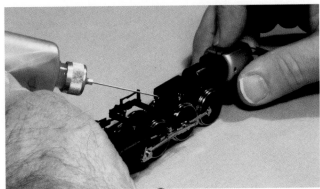

Step 3 Gearbox bearings

Place the Labelle no. 107 oil applicator at the point where the worm shaft passes through the front bearing of the gearbox. Gently squeeze one or two drops of oil into the bearing. Repeat this process for the rear bearing, being careful not to get lubricant on the flexible tubing located between the motor and the worm shaft.

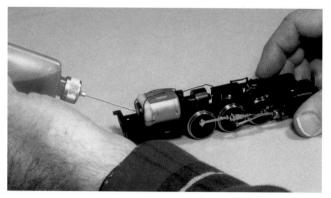

Step 4 Motor bearings
Apply one or two drops of Labelle no. 108 oil to each motor bearing. On most plastic locomotives you'll have to disassemble the internal weight castings to access the can motor. Once the weight is taken apart, place two drops of oil on the front bearing and one drop on the rear bearing. Don't over-oil the rear bearing as this can impact the locomotive's performance.

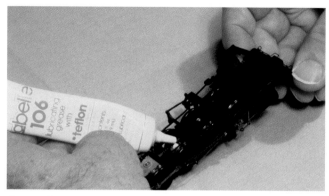

Step 5 Gear train
Grease the gear train with Labelle no. 106 white grease. This product contains Teflon and is ideal for acetal plastic gears or gear trains that combine plastic and metal gears. Squeeze the grease onto the gear and slowly turn the driver to coat the entire surface. After the locomotive is test run, the grease will work its way throughout the gear train.

Step 6 Driver axles
Lubricate the driver axles by either removing the cover plate and placing a drop of Labelle no. 108 oil on each axle bearing, or by pushing each driver to one side and placing the tip of the Labelle applicator on the other side of the axle and squeezing a drop of oil onto the axle.

Step 7 Final lubrication
Apply a drop of Labelle no. 108 oil to the shank of the hex-head crankpin screw holding the side rod to each driver. At the same time apply drops of no. 108 oil to the crosshead guides, each piston rod, the crosshead wrist-pin screw, and each rivet in the valve gear.

Step 8 Tender wheels
To clean tender wheels, use a variable speed motor tool with a ½"-diameter brass-bristle brush. Set the speed to slow and apply the turning brush on the wheel you want to clean while holding your finger at the other end of the axle. This technique works well for quickly cleaning wheels.

Labelle lubricants and uses	
Labelle no.	**Used for**
108 (light oil)	motor bearings, side rod screws, crosshead guides
107 (med. oil)	axle and gearbox bearings
106 (white grease)	plastic gears, plastic/metal gear combinations
103 (gear oil)	metal gears

Each of the major manufacturers of plastic steam locomotives uses a different assembly technique for its engines. While there are several companies producing quality plastic steam engines, for the purposes of this article, I'll focus on the disassembly steps for just three companies: Athearn, Bachmann, and International Hobby Corp. (IHC).

Athearn: Start by detaching the leading and trailing trucks. Then pull the front of the smokebox out of the boiler and carefully remove the light-emitting diode headlight that is plugged into a small printed circuit board.

Next, take out the large screw under the cylinder block. Then remove the brake gear by first popping the top of each brake hanger off its pin and pull the brake assembly out of the holes in the cover plate. Unfasten the screws holding the metal cover plate with a small Phillips screwdriver, followed by the screws holding the plastic cover plate. Lift off both plates. You now have access to the axle bearings and main gear.

If you want to remove the weight from the boiler, replace the plastic cover plate over the drivers, loosen the upper end of the cab handrails, and swing the railings away from the cab. Gently pry up the rear end of the cab and rock the front of it from side to side to lift it off the boiler.

Then find the two rectangular tabs that stick through the firebox under the front of the cab. Pull the bottom of the firebox outward free of the tab and lift the tab up with a screwdriver. Repeat this process for the other side. Pry up the back of the boiler with a small screwdriver.

Next, remove the ladders from the pilot deck by prying the locating pins out of their holes. Snap the short running boards off the exhaust pipes above the cylinders. Lift the back of

the boiler up over the top of the motor and slide it forward off the front of the weight. This takes a bit of force, so be careful not to crack the boiler.

Finally, remove the Phillips screws from the side of the weight, just behind the cylinders and from the rear inside the cab end. Lift the weight out of the plastic running-board casting to get to the idler gear. If you want to get at the motor, disassemble the two halves of the weight. The motor needs lubrication only every two or three years.

Bachmann: First remove the leading and trailing trucks by taking out the screws that hold them in place. Next remove the screw and drawbar and pull the deck ladders and boiler braces in front of the cylinders away from the boiler.

On the right side of the engine, pull the power-reverse lever away from the valve-gear crank and pull the back of the frame down and to the rear of the engine. The boiler will slide off the internal weight. Remove the screw just in front of the drawbar mount, and the top of the weight will separate from the drivers and frame. This will allow you to get at the axles as well

as the worm gear and its bearings.

If you need to reach the motor, remove the screws that hold the two halves of the weight together and slowly separate them. Make sure to catch the plastic washers that separate the halves of the weight.

International Hobby Corp. (Premier Series): Place the locomotive on its back in a cradle and detach the leading and trailing trucks, as well as the springs around the pivot screws. Then loosen the large screw under the cylinders and the Phillips screw in the center of the rear cab support below the cab deck.

Once the screws are removed, pull the back plate to the rear and lift the mechanism out of the boiler until the wires leading up into the boiler (for the headlight) are taut. Cut each headlight wire just in front of the vertical bronze strip it is soldered to—this will make maintenance easier. (This is also a good time to strip the insulation off the cut ends of the headlight wires and tin them so they can be resoldered to the bronze strip during reassembly.) Leave the boiler in the cradle, making sure that the weight hole for the cylinder screw and steel sleeve all line up.

NINE

Getting better performance from your MDC Shay

Improved electrical pickup is the key in S scale or HO

By Alexander Zelkin
Photos by the author

After modeling in HO for ten years, I decided to give Sn3 a try. Like many modelers who make the same move, I chose for my first project in the new scale to convert a Model Die Casting HO scale two-truck Shay kit to Sn3 using one of the V&T Shops conversion kits. The model looked great but once I started running it, I was disappointed with its somewhat sporadic electrical pickup. Here's how I made my MDC Shay run better by changing the way it picks up electricity. You can use the same technique for HO Shays.

Discovering the problem

When I converted the MDC Shay to S scale, I had every intention of running it, so I scratchbuilt a new gearbox and replaced the stock open-frame motor with a can motor. I went on to gather a few awards with my new baby, including the February 1986 Model of the Month award from *Model Railroader* Magazine. The only thing I didn't do to the Shay was operate it.

After moving in 1987 into a huge loft

with space to build my dream layout, I began operating my Shay on actual trackwork. The performance was not as good as I expected. In spite of the improved mechanical qualities, it was having problems with electrical pickup.

The stock MDC Shay picks up power through wipers that contact the backs of its eight wheels. If this contact is satisfactory, chances are the pressure against the backs of the wheels will create a mechanical bind. If you eliminate

Pickup shoes

Fig. I PICKUP SHOE MOUNTING

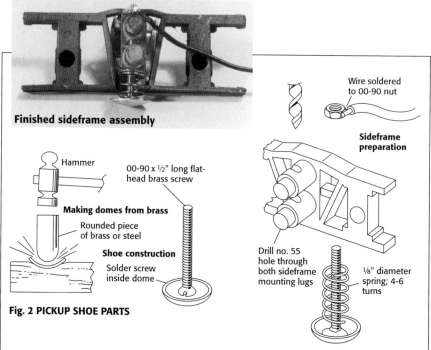

Finished sideframe assembly

Hammer

Making domes from brass

Rounded piece of brass or steel

Shoe construction

Solder screw inside dome

00-90 x ½" long flat-head brass screw

Wire soldered to 00-90 nut

Sideframe preparation

Drill no. 55 hole through both sideframe mounting lugs

⅛" diameter spring; 4-6 turns

Fig. 2 PICKUP SHOE PARTS

the bind, you lessen the electrical contact and it may go away altogether once dirt and dust gather between the wipers and the wheels.

After growing weary of constantly readjusting the wipers, I decided to come up with a more practical and efficient system: sprung pickup shoes.

I put pickup shoes between each pair of wheels on both sides of the trucks (see fig. 1). Since the shoes don't touch the wheels, I don't have to worry about any binds that may affect their rotation. The pickups are hardly noticeable and let the Shay crawl smoothly at the slowest speeds.

Cobbling some pickup shoes

To make the pickup shoes, you'll need four ½" brass 00-90 flathead screws, four brass 00-90 nuts, four small coil springs about ⅛" in diameter, a small sheet of .010" brass, and some thin electric wire to connect the shoes to the frame and motor.

Start out by removing the four side frames from the Shay trucks and drill a vertical hole with a no. 55 drill directly through the thicker part of both mounting lugs on each sideframe (see fig. 2). The 00-90 screw

must slide freely in the hole without being too loose.

From the .010" brass sheet, cut four little discs about ¼" in diameter. A hole punch works well for this. Figure 3 shows how to use a small hammer, a rounded piece of metal (brass or steel), and a piece of soft wood to pound the centers of the brass disks into a domed shape. Solder one disk to the head of each 00-90 flathead screw.

Cut four pieces of the small wire for pickup leads to the motor. The two rear wires can be shorter than the two front-truck wires. If you're in doubt about the length, leave them long and cut the extra length after the trucks are in place. Solder one end of each wire to a 00-90 nut.

You'll need four small springs about ⅛" in diameter and 4 to 6 coils long. I made my own springs but Precision Scale Co. springs no. 585-168 will work if you shorten them using wire cutters.

Assembly

Once all your parts are ready, slide each screw through a spring, then through the holes in the sideframe lugs. Add the wire and nut assembly

to the top of the screw to hold the pickup shoe in place.

Before putting the sideframes back onto the trucks, attach the two wires from the left sideframes to the metal underframe of the locomotive with 2-56 screws in no. 50 holes (see fig. 3). The wires from the right sideframes must be insulated from the floor and connected directly to the motor. The other motor lead is connected to the floor like the left sideframe wires. Push the sideframes into the sockets and check to make sure the shoes move up and down freely without catching in the sideframe holes.

Before running your Shay, carefully adjust the height and pressure of the shoes by rotating them. If the shoes are too high, you'll have poor electrical contact. Too low, and the spring's pressure on the shoe will be too strong, lifting the wheels from the rails and resulting in poor traction and slipping.

You may need to shorten the 00-90 screws above their nuts with a pair of side-cutting pliers to keep them from hitting the bottom of the floor.

Making the pickups isn't that hard and you'll be surprised with how well your Shay walks down the track with its new shoes.

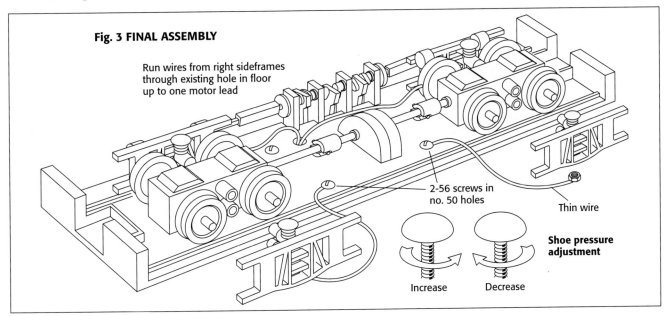

Fig. 3 FINAL ASSEMBLY

Run wires from right sideframes through existing hole in floor up to one motor lead

2-56 screws in no. 50 holes

Thin wire

Shoe pressure adjustment

Increase   Decrease

Better-running N scale switchers

Easy-to-add wipers for improved electrical contact

By Philip H. Mott
Photos by the author

What a wonderful feeling when your locomotives run well; what frustration when they don't. And it's really so simple, just a matter of maintaining electrical continuity from the throttle to the motor brushes. That's all, though it's often easier said than done.

Those neat little N scale 0-4-0 and 0-6-0 tank-type shifters are at a considerable disadvantage in this regard. Both pick up on only four drivers, and don't think for one minute that all four are doing their job through every second over every millimeter of track. When an engine lurches through a turnout, you just know that one or two wheels have lifted off the track.

And besides, even if all four wheels did maintain constant contact with the rails, there is still considerable current interruption at the six static frogs of a crossing. No wonder your timetable is all fouled up with late arrivals!

Here are a few model and track measurements to help us understand what we are up against:

Model Power and Life-Like 0-6-0Ts and Atlas 0-6-0 saddle-tankers have a distance of .875" between the front and rear drivers (the ones with the power pickups).

Some older turnouts on my layout have frog lengths as follows: Atlas no. 4s and 6s, .610" and Model Power no. 4s, .640". Obviously there's a major power interruption when little locomotives cross a plastic frog. When you consider that switching by small yard shifters should be done very slowly, matters get worse

The six frogs on two different makes of 15-degree crossings are all .610". However, and this is most significant, the live-rail distance between two frogs on a side measured .813" on a Roco and .870" on a Trix. This means that there is an instant when any of my 0-4-0s and 0-6-0s have two—and sometimes three—out of four pickup drivers on dead plastic. That ain't no way to run a railroad!

Solving the problem

These problems can be solved several ways. The best remedy would be to install turnouts and crossings with powered, all-metal frogs and make the necessary wiring changes. Another remedy is to convert the middle set of drivers to power pickups. This is an almost 100 percent cure, and here's a simple way to do it.

Figure 1 shows the underside of the plastic running board and the power pickups on a side-tanker. (Life-Like and Model Power are similar.) Mark a line .050" to .060" in from the edge of the wiper plate and score it with a few strokes with an

X-acto knife. Use an old X-acto blade for this job, but sharpen it first by honing it on a medium stone. This should produce a microscopic saw-tooth edge which will cut better on the pickup metal. Be sure to use a straight-edge guide. Don't attempt to cut clear through the brass at this point. Easy does it!

Next, starting very close to the rear rivet, score a mark for the final cut that will taper in from the edge to meet the first cut. Make a few strokes with the X-acto blade to have a well-defined groove.

Now ask your wife if you can borrow her very fine manicure scissors. Using these, make a series of tiny snips beginning at the tip end of the new third wiper to get the scored cut to separate. Gently see-saw the X-acto blade flat along the scored line, raising the thin strip as little as possible.

Now that you have separated the full length of the cut, make a slight sideways curve so the tip of this new wiper will ride on the center driver's tread, not on the flange as is the case with the original pickups.

Adjust the curve of the new wiper so it will have sufficient spring to maintain contact, but not so much as to create undue friction and overload the motor. If you have a magnifier and fine pointed tweezers, bend back the tip slightly to form a curved surface rather than a scratchy pointed end to ride on the wheel.

Shown in Fig. 2 is my method for converting the Atlas 0-6-0 saddle-tanker. This is an even easier conversion than the one in Fig. 1, with one important difference. The new wiper rides on the rim of the wheel, rather than the tread.

With minor surgery we have increased the current pickup potential on these locomotives by 50 percent. Even more importantly, we have now arranged for a center-to-center spacing of half what it was, greatly increasing the locomotive's chances of making it through to the end of the line.

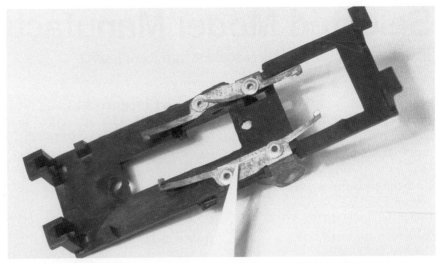

Fig 1 Improving the electrical pickup on this N scale tank locomotive is simply a matter of adding a third pickup plate on each side. These wipers contact the middle drivers and add them to the engine's electrical circuit.

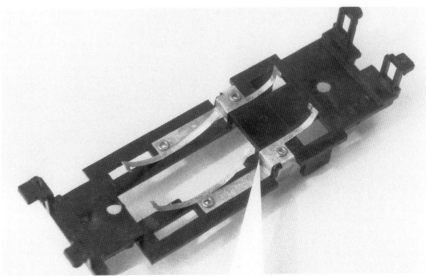

Fig. 2 (Middle and above) The author also modified this Atlas 0-6-0 saddle-tanker by creating a third set of wheel wipers. The job was even easier than for the locomotive in fig. 1.

Selected Model Manufacturers

(ready-to-run HO and/or N scale steam locomotives)

Athearn Inc
19010 Laurel Park Rd
Compton, CA 90220-6007
http://www.athearn.com

Bachmann Industries Inc
1400 E Erie Ave
Philadelphia, PA 19124-5698
www.bachmanntrains.com

Broadway Limited Imports
PO Box 376
Ivy, VA 22945-0376
www.broadway-limited.com

Con-Cor International
8101 E Research Ct
Tucson, AZ 85710-6758
all-railroads.com

International Hobby Corp
413 Allegheny Ave
Philadelphia, PA 19134-2322
www.IHC-Hobby.com

Kato USA Inc
100 Remington Rd.
Schaumburg, IL 60173-3705
www.katousa.com

Life-Like Products LLC
1600 Union Ave
Baltimore, MD 21211-1998
www.lifelikeproducts.com

Lionel LLC
50625 Richard W Blvd
Chesterfield, MI 48051-2493
www.lionel.com

Märklin Inc
PO Box 510559
New Berlin, WI 53151-0559
www.marklin.com

Model Die Casting Inc
5070 Sigstrom Ave
Carson City, NV 89706-2406
www.mdcroundhouse.com

Model Power
180 Smith St
Farmingdale, NY 11735
www.modelpower.com

Rivarossi
(imported by Wm. K. Walthers)